"At a time when a sense of purpose and authenticity are the strongly felt need of millions of people in the workforce, Joanne has written a guide that provides vital insights, even building blocks, to help people find their power. By shining a light on the lives and choices of so many different people besides herself—some leading in the public eye, and others quietly so—she has helped us understand that the path to purpose, whilst fraught with uncertainty, risks, and wrong turns, like any authentic quest, is a path worth taking. Reading Joanne's book is like being in conversation with those who've walked the path and can help us find our own way."

SACHIN MALHAN
Executive Director, Ashoka Changemakers

"Joanne masterfully weaves her own personal story with those of other leaders in the development world, extracting the essence of effective leadership—passion, a willingness to fight against inertia and old-think, and maintaining humility while acting with audacity. This is a wonderful primer, regardless of whether you are just starting your career, or looking to end it with a bang."

RODNEY FERGUSON
President and CEO, Winrock International

"What an inspirational, yet very practical read. I loved following Joanne's journey through her life and career, and realized so many commonalities that we share. I was particularly enchanted by: 'That being comfortable with the discomfort of not knowing what the future holds is actually a good thing.'"

SUSAN MCPHERSON
Founder and CEO, McPherson Strategies

T0026273

"Want a career with meaning, but don't quite know how to turn that passion into an actionable job hunt? *ChangeSeekers*—one part memoir, one part advice manual—brings you along for the ride on Joanne Sonenshine's journey from financial broker to corporate sustainability strategist. It will inspire and empower you to seek your own winding path to impact."

JEN BOYNTON
Editor-in-Chief, TriplePundit.com

"Joanne's story encourages each of us to seek a stronger presence in the day-to-day, question the status quo, and take risks to find the lasting impact for which we work tirelessly as sustainability professionals. Joanne's recommendations serve as a guide to anyone on a change-seeking journey."

LIZ MAW
CEO, Net Impact

"The human-interest stories expertly woven throughout this book are at once practical and optimistic. They lay an important groundwork, empowering readers to take on intractable social issues of our time."

CARRIE RICH
CEO, The Global Good Fund

"*ChangeSeekers* presents a personal appeal to readers to think deeply about the story they would like to be true for themselves, to work for that vision with manageable goals, and to open themselves to change, opportunity, and even disappointment along the way."

TONY SIESFELD
Managing Director, Monitor Institute

CHANGE SEEKERS

FINDING
YOUR PATH
TO IMPACT

JOANNE SONENSHINE

elevate

Published in Boise, Idaho, by Elevate, an imprint of Elevate Publishing.

Print ISBN- 9781945449178
eBook ISBN- 9781945449284
Library of Congress Control Number: 2016955890

For all of the difference makers improving our world; and the three biggest difference makers in my world: Dave, Jacob, and Daniel.

Contents

Introduction

In many ways both days felt the same, though the circumstances could not have been more different. In one case the world was burning, and my walls were crumbling down around me. In another, I felt my soul burning, any semblance of reason overtaking my feelings of anger and resentment. One could separate both experiences by years (12) or life events (going from single to married with two kids); one could even separate both days by maturity (age 25 versus 36, with travel, another degree, and a depth of professional experiences some could only dream of under my belt). The reality is that both experiences stemmed from the same realization about what makes people tick, the voracious hunger for truth, and an almost divine-like sense that an immediate change was the only way forward. Both days, September 11, 2001, and October 25, 2013, would be my 'diving off the deep end' points of inflection towards a path of personal and professional fulfillment based only on an instinct that each day shall be more meaningful than the last, and that the world is waiting for us to leave our mark.

—

At 1:46 p.m. on September 11, 2001, the "City" in London was bustling with bankers, flitting about like clones grabbing lunch before the New York financial markets opened just 15 minutes later. It was a perfectly crystal clear day in both London and New York, like an ocean of opportunity for the taking. I sat down at my desk and shoveled a few bites of my favorite curry into my mouth before sending my U.S. team the day's bond pricing.

I heard some news coming across the squawk box about a plane hitting the World Trade Center. I assumed a propjet clipped the top antenna of the building. I caught a quick glimpse of the gaping hole in the North Tower from the one television in our Managing Director's office, and my stomach churned. My desk mate grabbed my arm as he saw me turn white. "Are you okay?" he asked. My brain froze, and my first inclination was to call Dave. No answer. I started to panic as soon as the South Tower was hit. Our New York office couldn't be reached. I received an email from my Dad: "World Trade Center has been hit by a plane. Are you ok?" Then a second one: "Another plane has hit the Pentagon." I thought about everyone I knew in D.C. and New York and immediately shot emails off, checking on their whereabouts. My brain could not process what was happening, nor could I have imagined the reality of it all at that moment. Those of us in banking knew that Cantor Fitzgerald, with whom we had priced countless bond transactions, held offices at the top of the World Trade Center. There were others in our business who would surely be caught in the throngs of these attacks. It was impossible not to think the worst. The next half hour was a fury of email updates, Bloomberg news alerts, and frantic calls trying to reach family and close friends. I was blessed by the fact that my close friends and family were all safe and accounted for. Dave was on his way to class, but would return home when the city of Chicago thought it was being threatened too. So many were in worse shape than me.

That afternoon I sat in our Managing Director's crowded office to watch the towers fall on television. I still feel sick thinking about the helpless men and women who I saw jumping from the falling structures. I was the lone American in the room, and everyone treated me with kid gloves, knowing this day would transform my country and the future of our sanctity. I cried unabashedly.

As I sat there in complete shock over what was happening in my country, realizing that we were officially under attack by an unknown enemy, my office was evacuated. We heard that a plane had been hijacked in Amsterdam and was heading for the City of London. Fear ravaged me. I sprinted out of the office and found an overcrowded Tube with frantic Londoners. I spent the next few hours walking home from London City to my flat in South Kensington, where I hibernated for the next three days until my office reopened and the financial markets were up and running again. I felt shaken to the core for weeks, for months really. The days that followed made me numb. I had been shaken so badly by a sense that my land of liberty was now shrouded in a darkness I had never seen, nor could have imagined. September 11, for me, was like an awakening to the potential for evil, for fear, for an unbalanced world and a future unhinged. That day up-ended everything I had planned for my future, my success, my sense of hierarchy, and what impact I could have. Change was needed. This could never, ever happen again.

—

October 25, 2013, was a near-perfect fall day in Washington, almost as picturesque as that day had been September 11, 2001. I was putting the finishing touches on a presentation I would jointly give with my boss' boss at the nonprofit where I was then working. ("NGO," or non-governmental organi-zation, is another word for a nonprofit, so from here on I refer to that nonprofit organization as "the NGO.") I had been unhappy at the NGO for months, struggling with a lack of mobility, a sense that risk aversion was rampant across leadership, and a constant lack of challenge in my everyday work. I was bored, irritated, angry, and underutilized. Com-bined with a boss who micromanaged me and a leadership that seemed to condone favoritism, I was nearly at the end of my rope. I loved my work, and, in fact, yearned for more. I received praise for the work I delivered, especially by the corporate partners whose relationships I helped manage. Yet I could not seem to advance the work I was doing in any measurable way. I felt like my time was wasted. Like the chal-lenges I was trying to tackle every day—climate change, wa-ter health, food insecurity, poverty—were only getting worse. But I was helpless. Despite all of the years I spent to find my path to fulfillment, here I was with my soul crying in pity. It was burning in want. Why couldn't I do more, work harder, work smarter, get more done? I felt stymied and stonewalled.

But then October 25, 2013, happened. I had been working nearly non-stop on a proposal to one of the most valuable and longstanding corporate partners of the NGO, a company whose relationship at the time I happened to manage, and manage well, and after months of negotiating, we were nearly ready to sign. The presentation I was preparing on October 25 was the final element of delivery for the company's senior leadership, after which we expected to move forward into implementation.

The proposal process, in addition to taking months to complete, was rife with challenges stemming from internal politics that threatened to dismantle the relationship the NGO had taken nearly 15 years to build with this corporate partner. There was an overall lack of consideration among the old guard for new approaches and more innovative proposal elements, and despite my managing the corporate relationship at the time, I was continually doubted, questioned, and overlooked. No one seemed to take my interpretation of the corporate partner's interest to heart. I felt like I was tied between two ships sailing fast away from each other, my arms unable to stretch the distance. It was a paralyzing feeling, and I was disappointed that my time was spent managing the political differences within my organization, versus focusing on the impact of the work. I realized how little those around me saw the proposal as an opportunity to create lasting impact; instead the proposal was about "a win" versus the NGO's fear of failure. I felt my stomach sink over and over as I fought the internal battle, questioning which "side" was right and how to get heard over the politics and noise. The process nearly broke me, and I was worn down, emotionally exhausted, and questioning my future at the NGO.

Just days away from signing on the dotted line, I was working from home when I received a call from the boss' boss, fuming at me over the agenda for our corporate partnership meeting. He was furious that I had listed the attendees' titles wrong and demanded that I fix the agenda immediately. What the boss' boss didn't realize, despite me telling him time and again, was that this corporate partner had a distinct titling system that differed from most companies. I had the titles right. But he wouldn't have it. Instead, he hung up the phone. Without the courtesy of even listening, he hung up on me.

I felt a complete unraveling. The anger and frustration and demanding feeling that this work could be more meaningful if we cut the crap and focused on what is right for humanity at its core made me shake. Over and over in my head I kept thinking about what it would feel like to work on impactful issues without all the hierarchy and talking points, without all the political song and dance, based on truth and real connections, and transparency and respect for relationships and knowledge. I started to imagine a space to focus on the real issues plaguing our planet, a way to connect the "doers" and stop wasting my time with the "talkers." In my heart it felt true. That day after September 11 when I promised myself that change was needed, it was time to make that change and do it right.

My struggles with decision-making, authority, "inept" leadership, and a sense that my time was wasting away had followed me at every junction since I quit banking after September 11, 2001. Yet I had managed to keep up appearances, suck it up, and trudge on. But this time, my shell cracked.

My internal barometer for managing my own fury malfunctioned. I had no backing from my boss, no apologies from my boss' boss, and no end in sight to the madness. Had I reached the culmination of my career by working for an NGO with a mission I so believed in, or was there still more for me? Would I have to continue feeling dissatisfied by a lack of progress, or was there another path? Was this what I promised myself after September 11? That I would give everything I had to right the wrongs on this planet by arguing over a meeting agenda?

It was time to take back those years of hard work and devotion to my instincts and move forward toward building connective impact around all of us. Change was needed. Change was possible. And change would happen.

1

Which is Your Path?

Two of my closest friends, Joy and Karen, are marathon runners. Their dedication to training is remarkable. Four a.m. wake ups, long Saturday runs no matter the weather, personal bests, timed mileage, strength training, strange edible gels they eat to keep them nourished, the whole bit. What amazes me, in addition to their steadfast determination and dedication to the end goal, is the way they prioritize their training paths, their schedules, and their segmented goals.

I used to think that marathon runners could simply build up their endurance until they could easily run 26 miles and training would be over. In fact, I once started to train for a marathon, and had a running plan that took me from 3 to 20 miles in about 4 months. I never researched pace, timed segments, or those strange gels. I quit training to move to London in 2001, so I never got very far in the first place. I really had no idea that marathon running was instead about creating a series of individual races that you compete in sequence, adding up to the complete 26 miles at the end. For each component of the sequence, there is a time goal, a pace goal, a mileage goal, an emotional health and brain check goal, and a physical strength goal. It all seems so completely overwhelming to me, but my marathoner friends claim that this path to training is like any other goal you set for yourself—you create small milestones to keep yourself focused and ultimately you reach your finish line. I am amazed by their passion for the sport, their willingness to consume data in order to run a complete and successful race, and their strong emotional relationship to the training.

In discussing my sense of awe around what it takes to train for a marathon, Joy and Karen remind me that the way they think about marathon running is very similar to how I think about my career: My end goal to positively impact humanity can be met if I put in enough work, focus on small wins, and commit to enduring the peaks and valleys of the journey.

While I agree in principle that building an impactful career can be compared to training for a marathon, I ultimately compare seeking a path to fulfillment to the races one runs in a track and field competition. In most track and field sports, races are not just measured by start and finish; they may be measured by distance, combined with agility to leap hurdles, along with speed. These races combine multiple endurance tests in one, leading the participant to seek solutions to continuous physical challenges. There is a path that gets you from start to finish, but it includes so many elements that can trip you up. The test is to combine multiple skills, short spurts, long spurts, and a commitment to the long-term goal of being the fastest, most agile, lightest on your feet, and most physically successful. There is no right way to finish. The options to get from start to finish can be infinite, and the options for taking that path are endless. The same can be said for one's career.

Or perhaps one's path is more multifaceted. In her New York Times bestselling book, *Lean In: Women, Work and the Will to Lead*, Sheryl Sandberg commented, "Careers are like a jungle gym, not a ladder." As soon as I read that quote, I thought, "That is absolutely the truth!" We are inundated by the concept of a career as a singular path "up," from the lowest rung to the highest. Once you make it to the "top," there is nowhere else to go. Yet little is left for sideways exploration, or diversion to test creative outlets, or breaks to try new career trajectories. Success is measured by salary, title, years toiling at the same job, or decision-making authority. The vertical stepwise approach also excludes those who define success in the ruminations of life—being a successful parent, friend, sibling, daughter, or son; or those who travel the world, become enriched by cultures, volunteer, or teach. Success may not be linear for all. It can instead be more complex, multi-pronged, and full of risk-taking and adventure.

Finding a sense of fulfillment, or a way to make an impact on those around us, can take us down many paths, and those paths may be winding, circular, go backwards, or create multiple stops along the way. Each of us in our individuality has a different sense of where we most impact in our daily lives, our careers, our families, or the communities around us. The direction is not always perfectly clear.

Fulfillment may feel different for each of us, though the key is to find what drives us, and do our best to make decisions based on instinct. If we learn from our experiences, and understand that each twist and turn or shift in direction is neither a success nor a failure, but instead an opportunity to learn and experience toward our ultimate sense of fulfillment, we will be well served. This path can take years, or be uncovered in an instant. What was the right direction one day may be shifted in immeasurable ways the next. One must keep trudging through and see each experience as a reward in itself.

—

My journey has been nothing if not circuitous. Raised an only child by two middle/upper class parents from Shaker Heights, Ohio, who were born a mile apart from each other, went on their first date in seventh grade, and were high school sweethearts, I was always reminded about the importance of an open mind and education. My parents were wonderful parents, always supportive and never doubtful of my ability to succeed. We were incredibly close through the years, still are, and I share with them every element of my life. I am still influenced by them tremendously, and value their opinion highly. My parents have always been my biggest and loudest cheerleaders and I revel in the ability to impress them and make them proud. Any pressure I've felt over the years to excel, succeed, and find fulfillment was certainly not due to my parents, however. It was often due to my own vision of achievement—being a good student, being liked, and being kind.

There could have been other opportunities to find success as a child. Sports, art, dance, or music, however, were never my greatest strengths. I did have moments of grandeur as a field hockey player (I remember that one game where I played like I really "had" it. I made Varsity shortly after and never looked back), but that did not last very long. I was not an artist, quit playing every instrument I tried, and could have been a long shot at making it on Broadway after my eighth grade stint as Sarah Brown in *Guys and Dolls*, but I gave up on that too quickly. I was never an ugly duckling, but success was certainly not defined for me by my looks. As I grew older, I tried to define my success in being the "best" girlfriend (didn't work—I got jealous easily and needed too much reassurance), being the "best" cook (still trying to get out of the "average" category on that one), being the best "best friend" (only-children are tough to befriend—we don't like to share), being the "best" wife (I have definite moments of success here, but not always), being the "best" mom (always a work in progress), and so on and so on.

I started at private school in first grade after my Kindergarten teacher encouraged my parents to try private education where I would be more challenged. I thrived there, and have very good memories of my experience. The pressure I put on myself, however, made for some bumpy roads. Success for me was never measured in anything but high grades, teacher accolades, parent proud moments, and events like being selected for early admission to Northwestern University. Getting A's, being at the top of my class, being separated into the "advanced" math group, taking all AP classes by my Junior year, and testing into junior-level Calculus my freshman year at Northwestern (bad move—it was incredibly hard and I nearly failed) were my rewards. I felt glorified by the attention and praise, almost to a fault. I was hard on myself and grew disappointed easily if my grades fell or the teachers did not notice me excelling. The authority of teachers weighed heavily on me. If those who were "in charge" with high rank thought favorably of me, that had to mean something. That had to mean I was worthy, special, or successful. On the other hand, if they thought I was mediocre or not shining in my performance, it wreaked havoc on my psyche.

Take for example my junior year AP history class with Dr. Ross. He had a quiet, thoughtful presence, and I always felt a bit uneasy around him, as if, at any moment, I might blow my cover that my intellect was not worthy of his expertise. He was impatient with many of us, and seemed to find our side conversations catty. At first as a joke, and then in all seriousness, Dr. Ross started a tally of how many times each of us said "like" in the corner of the board as an indication of our unpolished speech. This was off-putting at the beginning, but over time it became a helpful reminder about what was appropriate and sophisticated. Even as an adult I try to think before I speak, hearing Dr. Ross' discerning voice in my head about how fillers in speech and writing show a lack of concentration.

Dr. Ross cared deeply about his students, and wanted us to do well, but lacked the delicacy in communication, often shaming us into succeeding. I respected Dr. Ross, but was scared of him, too. His authoritarian approach to reprimanding my writing made me struggle, and I felt failure on a regular basis around him. I abhorred writing assignments because

I simply could not excel. The thought of performing sub-par was petrifying.

Dr. Ross commented on each of my papers with every different version possible of "this is terrible." He grew impatient with me, and made it clear I was not easy to coach. I would go home in tears, mired in failure. I felt unloved by him. I handled his advice horribly. I was mean, angry, and disappointed that I could not meet his expectations. I took out my frustration on him often, and made it difficult for him to help me improve. My attitude was embarrassing, since Dr. Ross was trying to help, to guide, and to teach. It took me many years to understand how my struggles in performing for Dr. Ross were actually based on a fear of letting him (and myself) down. This fear would manifest itself repeatedly in different scenarios, with different figures of authority over time.

Dr. Ross, in the end, was an amazing teacher, winning "Best Teacher" awards year after year, because he did have a sense of who needed to be pushed to work harder, and how to reshape our thinking. He led his students to work above their comfort zone, and yet, despite an eventual realization that Dr. Ross was simply guiding me toward being a better writer, it took me a long time to realize that he was not trying to anger or upset me. He was encouraging me and challenging me in the only way that would work. He knew that I needed someone to test my feelings of self-worth in order to excel. It was something I did not see in myself at the time, but recognize regularly as an adult. My engagement with Dr. Ross was the first of so many experiences that humbled me, and would forever shape how I measured my relationship with those in authority positions, particularly those who simply knew more and understood more about how the world worked.

—

Traveling bumpy roads where I feel slightly unsettled with the status quo, or where I question decision-making, is what continues to propel me to find work that is most challenging, seems improbable, and takes arduous thinking. It's why I choose to work with Fortune 500 companies that have complex supply chains, and layers of demands to improve their mark on the world. Yet my path has been the opposite of linear. I still seek validation for good work. I want only the best, which to me translates to making the greatest mark on the world as one human can. Lofty? Sure. Feasible? Absolutely.

There are many times when I question my own decisions, too, or seem to move backwards instead of forwards in delivering meaningful work that positively impacts humanity. I have experienced a combination of sprints to the finish line met with long, painful timeframes of waiting and wanting more. My curved, winding path has led me to where I am today, owning my own company, dictating my professional future, yet I find myself still very much in an active mode of learning and questioning, letting my instincts and circumstances help guide me. I have learned to say "no" when needed, to be curious, to be brave. I continually am inspired by those people who are drawn to a path of fulfillment like a jungle gym, a series of sprints or hurdles, a circuitous, adventurous path toward finding true passion.

—

Senthil Nathan is one of these people. Senthil was born in 1982 to a coconut and rice farmer in a village of 300 people in India called Sithukkadu. Senthil's father had been one of eight children, born to a peasant farmer. As a young boy, the only people Senthil knew were farmers. Very few children attended school, and those who did went primarily for the free meal. Most of these children eventually dropped out, working instead with their parents on family farms. Senthil's father desperately wanted more for his children than he had as a boy. With one poorly run school in the village taught only in the local language, Senthil's father sought the best possible education for his son, preferably in English. He felt that only through education could Senthil help bring his family out of poverty and raise the standards for his own future. Senthil was constantly reminded that his mission was to bring that stability to his family, something he still thinks about daily.

Starting with seven other children that his father rounded up from nearby villages, Senthil was taught in English by a young high school graduate. His classroom, located in a cattle shed, was situated next to the cows. The school grew in size and stature, becoming well-respected among local villages. Over the years, Senthil kept his promise to his father and worked diligently through school and university, prioritizing education above all else. In 2004, he received his MBA and landed an entry-level operations trainee position at a ceramic vase factory, making just $12 a month. Although the earnings were meager, Senthil found living quarters and managed to support himself, not wanting to further burden his parents financially. His internal struggle to excel made him restless, and he was ready to "grow up in life."

The pressure by his father to succeed weighed on him heavily. After continuous searching, Senthil landed a business development job with General Mills. Influenced mostly by the opportunity to make more money and overcome the burden of his family debt, Senthil moved from General Mills to ConAgra in the space of a year, until PepsiCo hired him in 2006. Finally Senthil saw the trajectory of success, and within four years he was able to help pay off family debts, and contribute to his parents' savings for his sister's wedding expenses.

Over 10 years at PepsiCo, Senthil was promoted seven times, landing a role of General Manager for a territory covering 80 million potential consumers. He was making enough money to spend as he wished and live a good life. He made good on his promise to his father that he would work hard, be successful, help bring his family out of poverty, and live unburdened by financial uncertainties. Achieving these milestones were the highlights of his life. Until one Friday that would shift his path forever.

Senthil took the same commuter road into his office every day. He was used to children knocking on his car window, asking for money, begging for scraps. He often rolled down his window to give the children money, but would continue on to work as most do. One Friday a little girl knocked on Senthil's car window. Whether it was divine intervention, or something otherwise unexplained, Senthil pulled his car to the side of the road and asked the little girl where she lived. She showed him a temporary shelter in a slum covered in tarps and sheets nearby. Senthil was heartbroken and admittedly shaken. The next day, Saturday, Senthil drove back to see the girl. He learned that the families living there were all farmers, making little money in the rural villages, and were moving from town to town in temporary slums to beg for money, shine shoes, sell balloons, or anything that provided them food and additional income. Sixty children lived in the little roadside slum. That day changed Senthil's life forever. He asked the adults to gather their children each weekend for three hours at a time so he could teach them some basic language and math skills and provide them with quality food. Senthil continued this habit from his own volition for 18 months, ultimately starting a nonprofit to fund the activities.

It was this effort that shifted Senthil's consideration of what he wanted for his life. He realized that searching for meaning, and giving back to those who, like him, were mere farmers and needed help, was his calling. Despite disappointment from his family and some fear leaving a secure, well-paying job, Senthil left PepsiCo in 2015 to dedicate his life to solving the complex problems facing poor farmers.

I met Senthil when he flew into Washington, D.C., for a client meeting. Based in Bangalore, Senthil was in town to present to potential donors on the resource needs of his small farmer constituents and had traveled more than two days to join our meeting. He was likeable with a casual friendliness, putting me immediately at ease, and making it feel as we were old friends.

Senthil arrived into Washington at 4 a.m., and despite little sleep, he managed to join our meeting on time. Senthil's demeanor never shifted despite his clear lethargy. He was positive and happy, grateful to be a part of our engagement. Once our meetings finished, I offered to take Senthil on a walking tour, since he had not seen the White House, and he wanted some fresh air. As we walked the few blocks to Pennsylvania Avenue, I felt such joy exude from him, his eyes brightening as we approached the symbol of American freedom. We took a few pictures to mark the moment and proceeded to walk and talk and get to know each other.

I learned about Senthil's background and shared with him a bit about my own. I learned that Senthil questioned his future path, wondering whether there was more he could do with the skills and experience he had to develop more robust economic development solutions for poor farmers. He felt stymied in many ways by the burden he put on himself to solve a generations-long challenge of poverty.

While we discussed the different ways each of us was seeking a path to make an impact on the world, Senthil shared with me that he was leaving his current organization in 2017 to move to the United States and obtain a second graduate degree. Choosing among very well-respected schools, he was making his decision based on where he could afford the cost of living, and would likely rent an apartment so his wife and two children could stay in India and keep costs down. When I asked Senthil why he was willing to make such a big investment, he explained that, in the United States, we are able to express creativity, and experiment with innovative ideas. He sought an opportunity to learn from some of the greatest thinkers of his time, he said. He sees Americans having an opportunity to rise through one's life from his or her own merits, which he respects very much. He hopes to find a few individuals who share a common passion and want to find solutions to our global challenges. He hopes to build a social venture, and bring the right people to the table to effect real change. I have no doubt that he will do what he says, and the opportunity for Senthil to leave a meaningful mark on the plight of small farmers is ripe for the picking.

—

In many ways, Senthil's career path has had its peaks and valleys, taking him to the top as a corporate executive at one of the world's largest companies, and winding around through the tunnels of nonprofit work as he seeks the meaningful impact of giving back. The next path may be even more circuitous, with many unknowns ahead.

What I admire about Senthil is that the race to the top brought success to his family, delivered a lasting sense of comfort for his father, and helped Senthil deliver his promise that he would work hard and have a better life than generations before him. As if that was not enough, Senthil was full of desire to take on something different—to leave his comfort zone—and bring solutions to a community that so desperately needed him. He is someone who never once wavered in his quest to make a mark on his community, despite multiple hurdles. He saw the need to sprint fast at times, and stay steady at other times. His story inspires me, and his steadfast determination to try new experiences and challenge himself is a wonderful testament to his passion and personal mission.

BOTTOM LINE:

There is no one path to fulfillment. Your individual journey could be a marathon, a series of short sprints, or even several loops around the same track. There is no one way forward. What matters is that you always question where you are headed and why. Don't be afraid to challenge those in "authority" positions, and question everything. Be curious, be brave, and find your passion.

2
What Does it Mean to Have Impact?

When you wake up in the morning, are you the type of person who jumps out of bed, excited about what the day may bring? Or are you the type to drag yourself up, wishing for 10 more minutes of peace? Your answer may help determine whether you are inherently an optimist or pessimist. It may be surprising, but despite viewing circumstances as "glass half-full" versus "glass half-empty," we are all born optimists, with an innate ability to be helpful, kind, and empathetic.

In Felix Warneken's Harvard University study, "Precocious Prosocialty: Why Do Young Children Help?," he argues that the trait of being positive, helpful, and kind as seen in young children can be proven to evolve over time, and is, in fact, something we are born with. Warneken describes how this trait can be cultivated and developed with the right support and encouragement. There are also biochemical reasons for being kind, or for "doing the right" thing, and, as best-selling author and biochemistry expert Dr. David Hamilton has proven, "Emotional warmth produces the hormone, oxytocin, in the brain and throughout the body," which provides an overwhelming positive feeling.

Aside from a biochemical rationale for being kind or contributing to a greater good, many individuals have an unexplained, and in some cases, irrational, pull drawing them to circumstances that have a positive impact. Whether this draw is spiritual or otherwise, Dr. Hamilton also notes that compassion is biological, and thus is something that remains an integral part of human nature and our emotional makeup. So, what can be made of this innate element inherent in humans? And how can an individual with compassion, an overwhelming desire to give back, and optimistic instinct make real impact? What does that impact look like? How is fulfillment achieved once and for all?

Before September 11, I may have thought differently about this concept than I do now. In a twisted sense of irony, before 9/11 I had been voraciously reading about Middle Eastern history, religious zealots, and the history of fundamentalism. Having studied economics as an undergraduate, I saw market dynamics conflicting with religious freedom time and again, and struggled with why some populations could function well in a capitalist regime, and others could not. Societies immersed in religious strife often put the onus on their religious beliefs as the rationale for acting non-conformist.

As a part of this informal research, I read classic tales of good versus evil, and of heroes who contributed to a renaissance of art, culture, and trade by promoting a sense of community and family despite times of religious persecution or economic vulnerability. Poverty and power ping-ponged back and forth in non-functioning societies and the desperate sense of worthlessness made religious fundamentalism take hold. I was often left with questions about motivations.

In the case of most religious conflicts, was it really an *ideal* that led to brutality and massacre? Or was it about something more nuanced? Was it simply about lack of compassion? Or a malfunctioning support system to keep humans in check as it related to their innate interest in helping others? In economic terms, a breakdown in civilization could come down to supply and demand. Could it be an imbalance with too high of a demand for self-worth versus too little supply of opportunity that limited the level at which individuals focused on the greater good? Without equal footing, does compassion have a chance of existing? I noticed how some humans have taken kindness out of the equation, rather than build upon the instinctual chemistry that makes us compassionate beings.

The horrendous attacks of September 11 did nothing to quell my sense that some individuals have a complete lack of compassion, or that the kindness inherent in our chemical makeup is eliminated in extreme, unbalanced scenarios. When I made a commitment to seek change after that day, and ultimately find a way to bring compassion to those who most needed it, it led me to reevaluate my own sense of balance, and revisit where my own sense of goodness lay.

My daily life, which had revolved around a power-hungry and money-filled lifestyle, automatically felt tainted after September 11. An ephemeral dream, built on high salaries, prestige, first-class flights with my wealthy corporate bond clients, limo rides, champagne, and expensive suits, no longer seemed valid. I was thousands of miles away from my family, my boyfriend (now husband) was at his own crossroads, determining the future of his own career, and I had nearly abandoned him. I had friends reeling in grief after

9/11, and our world was turning on its head in the midst of a third world war threat thanks to the new "reign of terror." At once the promise of a bonus, the opportunity for promotion, and the first-class lifestyle were no longer important. Instead, I yearned for answers to the questions around what defines success, what drives impact, how we do better in this world for greater justice, and how humanity can truly prosper. It turns out I was not the first person to go through this metamorphosis.

—

Jaqueline Novograntz is the Founder and Executive Director of the Acumen Fund, an impact investment nonprofit working with "game-changing" companies to scale innovative solutions to our planet's most difficult challenges. This includes poverty, access to education (particularly for girls and women), sustainable housing, clean energy, and water. Acumen delivers basic services to very poor people via innovative partnership models, financing, and developing response mechanisms with local communities to lead them away from crippling poverty. Without question, Acumen has established itself as the most well-respected impact fund in development, and Novograntz as the esteemed and fearless leader working to address these global challenges.

I have admired Ms. Novograntz for many years, not only because of the groundbreaking way in which she has created a path to success for so many disenfranchised populations, but also because of the path to fulfillment she took, and the way she discovered her true compassion to deliver lasting impact.

The correlation between my story and the desire for change that I felt in 2001 is similar to that of Ms. Novograntz. In fact like me, Ms. Novograntz is an Economist and also started her career in the credit markets working for Chase Manhattan Bank in the 1980s. After three years at Chase, she yearned for a different path and sought to make an impact. Perhaps it was her introduction to the international financial markets during a period of time that was volatile and uncertain, and where poverty was rampant, contrasting with the wealth and greed of Wall Street. Perhaps it was a feeling from within that more was out there and she needed to seek a delivery of her innate ownership of kindness. However that pull evolved, Ms. Novograntz left her high-paying job to work in Africa as a consultant to the World Bank and UNICEF. Thereafter, she managed a series of microfinance programs before starting Acumen in 2001.

In her book, *The Blue Sweater*, a story about the interconnectedness among all humans and relying upon that bond to solve our greatest global challenges, Ms. Novograntz shares a piece of advice she received from a successful CEO of a healthcare company as she was just getting her microfinance programs off the ground at Acumen. To combat her apprehension, he said, "Just start...don't wait for perfection. Just start and let the work teach you. No one expects you to get it right at the very beginning, and you'll learn more from your mistakes than your early successes anyway. So stop worrying so much and just look at your best bets and go."[1]

What is beautiful about this is how real it makes the struggle to achieve true impact. The lofty goal of trying to solve poverty cannot be underestimated, yet the fear of failure can easily take hold, squashing the innate sense of compassion to right so many of our global wrongs. For Ms. Novograntz, her dream of changing the world initially felt like "falling flat on her face." She remarked, "They say a journey of a thousand miles begins with a single step. As a young woman, I dreamed of changing the world. In my twenties, I concluded that if I could only nudge the world a little bit, maybe that would be enough. But nudging isn't enough."[2]

I appreciate so much that Ms. Novograntz had an urge, perhaps innate, and likely shaped by her experiences in finance and economics, to seek fulfillment by using her knowledge and compassion to shift the trajectory of poverty. She did not give up when feeling like the path was too long, or too difficult, or as if she were falling on her face. She kept seeking her true impact, guided by the circumstances around her. The story of Ms. Novograntz is one that helps me understand how to shape our world for the better, and to create a human path for prosperity.

—

It can be hard to see your own path to fulfillment objectively. In fact it often takes strong moments, or ones that shake you out of your own monotony, to help you determine whether you have found what that impact can be, or whether you are far from it. Those moments can help redirect you down a different path, and challenge your inner voice to make a change. I have no doubt that my search for fulfillment and hope for making an impact is based on exploring humanity's greatest strengths. And this exploration for me has only just begun. Yet thus far my winding, circuitous, and, in some cases, nonsensical path has helped me understand that actively looking for a means to an end is not productive. The cliché about the journey being more important or meaningful than the destination holds true for me. I pleaded with myself for years to find meaningful work, to give back, to make lasting change, and grew impatient if I felt I had not landed in the right place to do exactly that. In some cases I should have recognized that the "change" I was seeking was in force all along. I desperately needed my crazy journey to look back and see it for myself.

Fulfillment and lasting impact are not easily measured, nor are they easy to find. There is no roadmap, and there are few resources available to help direct. Within me, I had to focus on several personal development actions, and take several risks, before I could find what it was that would truly inspire me as a career and for personal fulfillment:

1. I had to stop being the person I thought I was, and embrace the person I needed to be. This meant giving up on a dream I thought I had, but was clearly not providing me the personal satisfaction I craved. September 11 had a lot to do with redirecting my priorities and helping me redefine my personal and professional intent. Later in my career, I was able to redirect my focus and energy without such drastic consequences. Understanding that dreams change and evolve is tough in the beginning, but freeing in the end.

2. I had to learn how to follow my instincts. I have always been a "go with your gut" decision maker, and tend to know pretty quickly whether a choice is a good or bad one. That does not always translate into effective decision-making, since I also tend to be a bit rash. As I have grown from both personal and professional life experiences, I've become more in tune with my own instincts, not second-guessing myself, and not concerning myself with what others say. This is clearly a symptom of maturing, but is not always easy to do. It has taken a lot of practice and confidence building to get to this point. This leads to number 3:

3. You must have the confidence it takes to stop questioning yourself. When you spend most of your life feeding off accolades, but do not believe in yourself, you will not be able to find your own fulfillment. Being successful at self-direction on a path toward true impact means finding the confidence from within to take risks, make mistakes and apologize for failures, and move on without second guessing yourself. This takes experience, knowledge gathering, and practice, but for me the only way I've been successful in advising corporate leaders is by staying true to what I know, not questioning myself, and trusting my instincts.

Lucy Helm is someone whose trust in herself and her ideals has inspired me. Lucy is an executive vice president, general counsel and secretary at Starbucks Coffee Company in Seattle, Washington. Before joining Starbucks, Lucy was a trial lawyer and disability rights advocate. I originally met Lucy in January 2012 on a trip organized by Starbucks in Costa Rica. I had been supporting an element of my NGO's partnership with Starbucks, and joined the Costa Rica trip to share details about that partnership to a group of its staff. Lucy was attending to learn more about the complexities of coffee origin community development, operations, and environmental sustainability, and happened to be on my bus. I remember Lucy being incredibly humble, open to learning, curious, and respectful. Being general counsel at one of the world's largest companies had clearly not squelched the values so important to this girl from Kentucky.

We met again in Guatemala in November 2014 on a trip Lucy joined as part of her Board of Directors position with the global humanitarian and development organization, Mercy Corps. Lucy was visiting one of the food security projects run by the Guatemala Mercy Corps team, and also partially funded by members of the coffee industry. Lucy had joined our trip of her own volition, and simply to understand better how Mercy Corps ran its projects. I had joined the trip as part of an engagement I had with a coalition of coffee companies, working collaboratively to improve food insecurity in coffee-growing regions. Several of the companies involved were also on the trip, in addition to Starbucks. The trip was arduous, involving six- to eight-hour jeep rides up and down dirt-paved mountains. The recent tropical storms had nearly decimated the landscape, and homes had been destroyed from the mudslides. We trekked through very difficult terrain, and Lucy never once complained. In fact, she smiled and stayed positive the whole time.

During our time together in the Jeep, we spoke of our childhoods, and Lucy asked me a number of questions about my path to starting my own consulting company. She asked about the work our coalition was leading, curious to understand the role a corporate leader like Starbucks could have in reshaping the poor among its coffee growing communities. Lucy was every bit as human and vulnerable as the rest of us, as we spoke with local farmers about the challenges they face growing coffee, making a respectful livelihood, and managing large families and land that were responding unfavorably to dynamic environmental conditions.

Being together in Guatemala, seeing firsthand the gut-wrenching outcomes of poverty, was a way to build an automatic bond between all of us traveling together, as these types of trips often do. With Lucy, I felt an immediate connection to her personal mission, which I learned has been for many years to have a meaningful impact on the world wherever she could. As it turns out, Lucy has spent her entire adult life giving back, volunteering as a board member with the Washington YMCA Youth & Government Program and on the advisory board of Disability Rights Advocates, a nonprofit disability law center in Berkeley, California. She has been a longtime advocate for the rights of persons with disabilities, veterans, youth, and the homeless, working with other Starbucks leaders to build successful programs giving back to these and other often-disenfranchised populations.

Lucy admitted that she never saw herself working for a for-profit company, since in her heart she wanted to work for a mission-driven organization that prioritized community investment and societal improvement. After being a trial lawyer, she assumed that finding that sense of fulfillment would only come from working for a nonprofit. As it turns out, Starbucks has a values system that is based largely on the very values Lucy was seeking to deploy, and thus she chose a path that was very different from one she had originally envisioned for herself. The outcome is that Lucy has been able to positively impact so many different types of communities in her role.

At the end of our trip, Lucy and I agreed to stay in touch. I assumed as busy as general counsel at a Fortune 100 company would be, I may never hear from Lucy again. But, lo and behold, when I sent my first email that I would be in Seattle in early 2015, Lucy asked me to join her for coffee. I was so touched, and we had a lovely visit, catching up on Lucy's activities with Mercy Corps, and sharing updates on our respective work. I saw Lucy again in the summer of 2016, and shared with her my plans to write this book. I asked her if she could expound a bit on what her path to fulfillment has looked like, since it has taken her on a journey she had not originally planned for herself. She thought for a long minute, and then said without hesitation that it is possible to achieve impact no matter what you do, or where you are. She shared that one must look for that opportunity to shift the status quo, seek it out if necessary, but that there are ways to make changes in all we do, in every role we have, and in every environment in which we live, work, and play. For Lucy, she had assumed that working in a nonprofit environment would be the only place she could make a difference. And then she found Starbucks—an organization that built the concept of effecting change into its core values. Now every day Lucy can make a positive impact as a senior leader at one of the world's most influential companies, and continue to find ways to give back as a volunteer among other organizations. She took a risk down a different path, but found her impact.

—

Like Lucy, I had a path I envisioned for myself as a young woman, and yet had not considered the multiple ways I could effect change or seek fulfillment. After an exploration of more than 15 years, and experiences grandiose, strange, powerful, and mundane, I have started to find the answers to the questions around what defines success, what drives impact, how we better this world for greater justice, and how humanity truly can prosper. By no means do I see an end to this search, and in many ways I see my career path as my life's work, in addition to the legacy I leave for my children. The challenges we face as humans, day in and day out, are complex, severe, and, at times, incredibly scary. Yet the risks we take are what make it all worthwhile.

BOTTOM LINE:

Making a difference means different things to different people. Everyone finds their fulfillment in different ways, at different speeds, and through various journeys. You may find that what you were looking for all along was the purpose of the journey in the first place. Follow your instincts, trust yourself, and find the confidence to test assumptions.

3
Who Do You Think You Are?

Each of us lives under the weight of expectations, either those we set for ourselves, or those placed upon us by others. The pressure of expectation can feel consuming, since it demands deliberate action. The origin of the word is even fraught with a sense of "what if," derived from the Latin word *expectationem*, meaning "an awaiting." As we manage expectations about our future path, what is it we are "waiting" for? Is there a statute of limitations?

When I was a little girl, I vividly recall playing office in my backyard, answering phones made of rocks and filing blank envelopes. I wanted to be a "business woman" when I grew up and set my course accordingly. I had an image of what that looked like: me as an important, high-powered, and in-demand boss. As I grew older, and gained experience, my expectations were aimed high and I had no patience for "waiting." I learned quickly, however, that one must "pay her dues," waiting to be told what to do and how to do it.

I began to wonder when I would get to make the decisions. I was anxious, determined, and ready.

Who you are, and ultimately who you become, is built on multiple layers of expectation. Yet shouldn't your path be based not on what is expected of you, or what dues you have paid, but instead on where you see need, where you can provide value, and ultimately where you can have the most impact?

—

Michael Jones is someone who did the absolute unexpected after he left his multi-million dollar company and entered the coffee business. In 2014 I met Michael, founder and CEO of Thrive Farmers, a coffee company based in Atlanta, Georgia, at a coffee trade show. I had read about Michael's story in Forbes[3] the month before and had to hear more. He was quoted saying that when he was younger he "...*thought that money, fame and success would be the solution to everything*." When I asked him about that very typical sense of expectation, Michael shared with me that so much of his identity as a young man was based on the belief that what he accomplished had a direct correlation to who he was as a person. He believed that his identity was defined by his net worth, his successes in business, and his material possessions.

Growing up in a blue-collar, middle-class family in central Georgia, Michael quickly realized that he wanted a life different than his parents. From a young age he was fascinated by the way in which the "rich" people of the world lived. He began to set goals for himself, initially deciding he wanted to start a company that would land on the INC Magazine list of the 500 Fastest Growing Companies. Michael launched himself into serial entrepreneurship, with the sole goal of landing the perfect life living rich and powerful.

After a series of business starts and stops, Michael settled at the helm of a highly successful healthcare company, eventually landing at No. 138 on the INC 500 list. Michael's company was also listed in the top five of Forbes' America's Most Promising Companies list by 2011, another goal he had set for himself early on. Michael admitted that, despite the accolades, the feeling was "hollow." *"This period of, 'chasing shiny stuff,'"* as Jones refers to it now, *"seemed transient, and lasting satisfaction kept slipping through his fingers."* With faith acting as a driving catalyst in Michael's life, he realized that all the success and accolades were simply temporary, and he needed a new direction to find "eternal significance."

Shortly after this period, Michael took a break from working to reflect on what he wanted out of his life. He told Forbes he wanted the next phase of his life to be about adding "value." He told me he was seeking a fulfillment he had not yet experienced, a way to have impact for his children and those around him.

At the time, Michael's father-in-law was a coffee farmer in Jamaica, and had shared with Michael the challenge of making coffee profitable, given how little exporters paid per pound. With added time on his hands, Michael began to research the extreme volatility of coffee prices. He was shocked to learn how little farmers received for their coffee, despite how much stores charged for a bag of beans.

Through his research he learned that small farmers—those with just a few acres of land—were struggling to make ends meet, and were greatly stressed by frequent changes in price. Challenges around access to healthcare, nutritious food, and adequate shelter were rampant. Seeing firsthand the poverty amidst the small coffee farmers that grow the bulk of the world's coffee, Michael was convinced there had to be a better way. He realized he could use his business prowess and experience, as well as his unique calling to find a more meaningful path, to fix the broken coffee industry. Together with co-founder and lawyer-turned coffee farmer, Ken Lander, Michael Jones created a revenue-sharing program that stabilizes price through long-term agreements, making coffee farmers real partners in their own business.

Ken's path to fulfillment was also laden with twists and turns, as he left the high-powered and lucrative world of litigation to grow coffee in Costa Rica. He sought a simpler, more peaceful environment for his family, and bought a small farm in Monteverde. He planted coffee trees, among other crops, living off money from several real estate investments back in the States. The economic turndown of the early 2000s caused Ken to lose significant wealth, and his small plot of land was all he had left. He started roasting and selling coffee to tourists and other passersby near his town, and was suffering from the same price challenges as Michael's father-in-law. A friend, familiar with Ken's story, introduced him to Michael. Shortly thereafter, Thrive Farmers was born.

In August of 2016, as Michael and Ken continued to drive home the notion that a company can coexist with a social mission and profit aim, Thrive landed on INC's Top

500 list at No. 19. Michael's realization that the impact this accolade has on coffee farmers and their families has allowed him to feel far more joy than his first time around on the list. Both Ken and Michael are driven by strong faith, and a belief that they can change the world one cup of coffee at a time. They are dedicated to giving to others as a key tenant of Thrive Farmers' work. I am humbled and inspired by their search for greater meaning and their dedication to a path that was not initially in the cards for either of them.

—

Like Michael and Ken, I started my career on a path to expectation. I was going to be a stockbroker.

—

My interest was piqued as a high school junior by an economics elective. I learned about the basics of supply and demand and the workings of the stock market. Each of my classmates selected a stock to follow in the newspaper every day, tracking pricing and volume. At the end of the semester, my stock had outperformed everyone else's, and I felt a unique sense of accomplishment. I carried that excitement into my senior year, when I decided to volunteer at a brokerage firm in downtown Cleveland for my senior project. For three weeks, I filed stock orders on pink slips of paper for the Securities and Exchange Commission. The electricity of the trading floor hooked me. The mostly white men in suits seemed so powerful, transacting large sums of money while sitting in leather chairs and activating buttons on their trading screens. Their lives seemed romantic.

The energy ran on the trading floor from market open to close. The notion that finance and banking could take me on a path to superiority convinced me to spend the next two summers interning at the brokerage firm while in college at Northwestern. I eventually landed at the bond desk, where I was responsible for managing inside communications between the bond salesmen and their traders. It felt like a real job and on the path to expectation, I was paying my dues.

By the end of my junior year of college, I knew that, with one more year before graduation, I had two options before me: Either I could become a consultant like most other Econ grads, or I could become an investment banker on Wall Street. The answer was obvious, with Wall Street being the easy winner. The competition for jobs was fierce, though, and summer internships were no exception.

The beacon on the hill in banking for me was Goldman Sachs. The gold letters and austere lobbies, the glass-enclosed offices and mahogany conference tables. The cufflinks, packed trading floors, and power lunches. It all sang to me and lulled me into a vision of my own future, clothed in designer suits, and shaping financial markets by developing unique hedging tools. I was thrilled by an offer to intern at Goldman in downtown Chicago the summer between my junior and senior years of college. I was introduced to the leaders of each division, treated to free lunches, and got to wear fancy clothes and pretend I was a big shot. But I wasn't. I worked for Goldman Sachs Institutional Funds and spent my entire summer filing customer statements. It was excruciatingly boring, totally unglamorous, and taught me nothing about finance or banking. What I learned that summer, though, was far more valuable than anything I could have learned by trading bonds.

During one of our lunch presentations, we received an introduction to the Fixed Income Sales team. The boss of this team, let's call him Richard, was larger than life, personable, and hilarious. He represented everything I aspired to. He offered us the opportunity to sit with him on the trading floor and observe him and his team. That invitation was my opening, and I spent my lunch hours with Richard and his team as often as I could. I was their adopted intern, though I could not technically do much work for them.

While I was filing 7.5 hours of the day with the Mutual Fund team, I spent the rest of my time pretending to be part of the sexy Fixed Income Sales team. I was living my dream. I felt successful and powerful. I got to know the guys on the Fixed Income Sales desk well. I asked them about their families, their professional histories, and their lives. I heard about luxury boxes at the Cubs games and after-work drinks at the Four Seasons. The technical nature of fixed income sales started to seem accessible, too. The learning curve became a little less steep. That summer I got a unique view into what I thought was the real working world, and into a sense of humanity I thought I wanted. These guys were working hard, making money, and being successful. I left Goldman in utter love and on a complete high.

Richard promised me he would do everything he could to get me hired full-time after I graduated. It was as close to a done deal as could be imagined. Goldman had an entry-level analyst program for which I was interviewed, thanks to Richard. I was asked back for a second interview, waving hello to all of my old friends, and was forced to sit in the waiting room for about a half hour. It turns out the 30-minute wait was part of Goldman's modus operandi. They wanted to test your patience and strong will.

The second interview was highly technical. I struggled with some of the math, and felt completely out of my element. I wanted to tell the recruiter that each of the guys on the Fixed Income floor could vouch for me—just go ask them! That this math was inconsequential. This was my path! This was my expectation! It didn't matter. In the end I did not get the job. My standard rejection letter was as close to an actual stab in the chest as I could possibly envision. I was devastated. Richard said he did what he could, but that the candidates that year were far superior—all from Ivy League schools, all could speak three languages, had traveled the world, and majored in Math, Chemistry, Hard Interview Math Problems, who knows? I was left amazed that, despite my familiarity with the business, the value I could add to Richard's team, and my time spent at Goldman, I was passed over, my dues still not paid.

Since I was graduating in just a few short months, I had to find a job. With high expectations for myself, it was trying on my psyche and ego. The rejection from Goldman was a tough lesson in managing my pride and expectations. The vision of myself in power suits, managing complex hedging portfolios, shaping the future of financial markets seemed to fade quickly as I received more rejections from all of the big (and little) banks. Shouldn't I be working for an organization that got "me," where I could deliver good work and be a strong team member, rather than be just another number cruncher? I learned quickly that the answer for many of these organizations was "no." What mattered to the Goldmans of the world was not how creative I was, or how easily I could talk to potential clients, or how much of an advocate I would be for the brand, but how I did a task, answered a direct question, and completed a math problem.

The continuous rejections my senior year were emotionally draining and painful. But without question the job search process ingrained in me a feeling of, "if it's not meant to be, it's just not meant to be," that I had to learn to live with. It also helped me manage my own expectations, though I was still impatient to reach that visualized image I had created for myself.

By spring of my senior year, I received a modest job offer from a Dutch investment bank with its North American headquarters in Chicago. I would not be moonlighting on the Fixed Income Sales Desk, nor would I be manning the trading floor. Instead I was entered into a training program that would teach me the workings of the investment bank and eventually settle me into a full-time position on a "to be determined" desk matching my skills. I was relieved to have a job, and knew I would make enough money to live a very comfortable life right out of college. Yet I was slightly disappointed that my Wall Street was actually Randolph Street, a few blocks from the Chicago Loop. My expectations were squashed, but I kept my eyes on the prize, which was to get back to that Fixed Income Sales Desk.

—

The summer after graduation I traveled to Eastern Europe by myself. I fantasized about having the time to think and prepare for the next steps after college. I loved the idea of operating on no one else's timeline but my own, to visit museums, take long walks, and revel in the peace. I bought an unlimited train ticket with a plan to see as much as I could in three weeks. Toward the tail end of my trip, I was leaving Salzburg, Austria, en route to Budapest, Hungary. My train left at 9:10 a.m. and I arrived as the train was leaving the station. Like a moment from the movie Sliding Doors, I watched my train leave as I sprinted to make it.

As I waited three hours for the next train, I internalized my frustration for leaving the hostel 10 minutes too late, and blamed myself for not sticking to the schedule. As I climbed the stairs to my next train at noon, I noticed empty seat after empty seat, until I spotted a backwards baseball hat and heard an American accent. "Hi guys," I said to the two frat boys sitting together in the middle of the car. "Hey," they said back. Since no one else was joining us on the train, I took the seat across the aisle from them and introduced myself. "I'm Jeff. And this is Dave."

As the train pulled away from the station, I learned that Jeff and Dave were old friends from Columbia, South Carolina, and had just graduated as well. They were traveling for a few weeks before Dave moved to D.C., and Jeff back to Columbia. Thinking I would never see them again after we arrived in Budapest, I spun on my heels and started off on my next adventure. The next day, as the rain started to fall, I saw Jeff and Dave walking toward me on a side street, and I waved them under an awning to stay dry. Small world, we said, in seeing each other again. One more time we bid our goodbyes, our 'nice to meet yous' and headed on our respective ways.

My final day in Budapest, I was leaving a museum, and saw Jeff and Dave walking in as I was walking out. How strange, I thought, that I kept running into them! It was too many times to be chance, surely. Fast forward a week, and I was in Prague meeting up with some friends who were on their own travels. Sitting outside during breakfast, I caught a glimpse of what looked to be Jeff and Dave walking toward me. In Prague! A week after I saw them for the last time! "What are you doing here?" I asked. I learned that the boys' plans had changed due to a small mishap with Jeff's passport. By that point, our continuous meetings started to signal a fate of some kind, so the three of us spent the day together.

Under the haze of a few rounds of Budvar that evening, Jeff and Dave convinced me to travel with them to Amsterdam for the last few days of my European adventure. I agreed and the next morning we set out on a 14-hour train ride into the Netherlands. During that time, while Jeff mostly slept, Dave and I talked. We talked about our families, what we hoped to achieve in this next phase of our lives, past relationships, and friendships. We shared with ease, and I swooned over the comfort I felt around him, as well as the way he made me laugh so effortlessly. I left Europe with a nagging feeling that this goodbye, like the others, would not be the last. I would be right.

By the end of that year, Dave and I were traveling back and forth to visit each other, and I managed to find an opening on the Chicago Fixed Income Sales Desk at the bank. Dave left Washington to join me in Chicago and start law school.

Nearly a year later, in the spring of 2001, I received a call from our team leader, who was based in London. He asked me to find a quiet location and call him back. When I did, he asked me if I would move to London to take over as Associate on the London Fixed Income Sales Desk. This would include a promotion, expenses-paid move, a flat paid for by the company, and so on. My jaw dropped open and my heart started beating fast. I wanted to immediately scream "YES!" but I hesitated. What about Dave?

At once my path towards highest expectations had a kink. The path was not just about me anymore. Dave and I were serious, and were likely going to get married. How could I leave him and move to London? That night I cried with Dave for hours. He knew I desperately wanted the opportunity to live in the international center of banking, and carry out a dream, deliver the image I had set for myself as a young girl. Yet leaving him and moving half way around the world was not fair to either of us.

After deliberating for several days, consulting my family, friends, and having desperately sad conversations with Dave, I decided to take the offer and move to London. It was something I had to do for me. I had to prove to myself that this path of expectation I had set for myself was achievable. It tore my heart out, but I had to do it. This position was everything I had thought I wanted for myself.

—

At the same time I was moving my life across the Atlantic, I was watching closely the career changes of a man who I emulated and related to. Robert Rubin, who was Treasury Secretary of the United States under Bill Clinton, retired political office in 1999, and slowly re-entered the world he had known for most of his adult life: Wall Street.

Born in 1938, Rubin trained as a lawyer and had spent most of his career at Goldman Sachs. As one of Goldman's most well-respected and admired leaders, Rubin nearly single-handedly built it into one of the most influential players in the options trading business. Rubin's name was synonymous with success, both within the confines of Wall Street and eventually the White House. I watched Rubin's actions as Treasury Secretary carefully, since my job within Fixed Income Sales depended heavily on which way the Treasury markets moved. I found his policy work meticulous, fair, and amazingly collaborative, as he managed close relationships with Federal Reserve Chairman Alan Greenspan, Deputy Larry Summers, and President Bill Clinton.

Rubin's description of market movements was straightforward, transparent, and clear, and in many ways I felt this made me better at my job. Rubin dealt with his fair share of criticism, but he did so with grace and class, and never seemed to fall under the weight of political maneuvering.

Around the same time I moved to London, Rubin was contemplating his return to banking. In his memoir, *In an Uncertain World: Tough Choices from Wall Street to Washing-*

ton, Rubin opines on the path that led him from Wall Street to Washington, and the thread that brought both together. Rubin's theory throughout is that even with the best information or laid plans, nothing is ever fully certain. His tone is one of humility, recognizing that decisions are wrought with imbalance and risk. In one passage Rubin discusses motivation and expectation. He cautions that for those seeking fortune, fame, or power, one must consider fulfillment as well. For jobs come and go, but finding true satisfaction in life is much harder. Rubin shares that many young men and women whom he met at Goldman, or while working in the White House, were looking for a path to money or titles, yet found years later that no amount of wealth or authority was truly satisfying. He remarks, "the only place people find fulfillment is within themselves,"[4] and that thought buried itself in the back of my conscious for a decade, comforting me at pivotal times. Rubin rejoined the financial markets from 2007 until 2009 as acting Chair of Citigroup.

I met Robert Rubin at the D.C. airport shortly after I read his book, and told him how much I appreciated his honesty and insight. He was kind and gracious, and thanked me for approaching him.

—

As Rubin was exiting the White House, I was facing my new life in London. On paper it was everything I had expected for myself years before. My fantasy about working on a trading floor, with the most powerful bankers in the world, the power suits, the money, and first-class lifestyle had come true. I was 25 years old, with a high-profile job, six-figure salary, flat in South Kensington, and was traveling to some of the most beautiful cities in Europe. I was climbing the ladder, working on a Sales Desk with revenue that dwarfed the Goldman office in Chicago. I could only look forward, not back. But there was a problem. I was miserable, felt like a fraud, and wanted out.

BOTTOM LINE:

Expectations can lead to feelings of frustration, dissatisfaction, and regret. You design your path based on the expectations of those around you, but it should be based equally (and maybe even more so) on what you feel, where you see need, where you provide value, and where you can have the most impact.

4

How Circumstances Change
Your Path

When everything you think you want becomes undone, it is terrifying. The risk you take to reshape your life is where the beauty lies.

—

Working 60- to 80-hour weeks while trying to make a life for myself in London was unsustainable. The little free time I had I was either flying back to Chicago to visit Dave, or trying to stay in touch with friends and family. I managed to sightsee and travel to a few new cities over long weekends, and in small slivers of time I tried to make new friends and create a routine in my new neighborhood. I never felt fully committed, though. I felt far away and alone.

While living in London was an opportunity of a lifetime, I knew I was not taking advantage of the opportunity nearly as well as I could. I was originating hundreds of millions of dollars of bonds for very large companies, and, in doing so, engaged with exceedingly wealthy clients, most of whom treated us bankers like shit. Sure, we could enjoy a few good meals here and there, and the wine poured freely, but we were robots, not humans, there only to close the deal. I saw so much money flow through the financial markets that it started to jade me. Only a $200 million deal was worthy of our time. Anything less became a burden to our traders.

One of the weekend trips I took was over a four-day weekend. I had asked a few colleagues where I should go that was still untouched by Western civilization, but where I would be safe as a single woman traveling alone. I had a yearning to explore and see a part of the world that was new to me. I felt the need to be grounded in a greater sense of reality than the one in which I was living. I ended up in Turkey. It was the farthest I had ever traveled.

Istanbul was beautiful in its rich culture and history. The tradition of Muslim call to prayer was still very pertinent in daily life, and the bells rang loudly five times a day from the famous Hagia Sophia mosque. The Bosphorus was an emerald blue, the food fresh and flavorful. I was taken to a rug shop, served tea, and told tales about the owner and his family as if in a storybook. I visited the souk and bartered over jewelry and art. I felt fully removed from my reality, and instead supplanted in a land before time. Nothing prepared me, though, for such stark poverty. I had seen poverty in American cities, and knew that homelessness was a challenge across the globe. But to see small gypsy children begging for money on the streets ripped my heart out.

Coming back to my London flat felt unfair, and the opulence I experienced all around me in my investment banking world sickened me when considering how the poorest of the poor were living. I started to grapple with existential questions regarding wealth, and began reading about the economics of poverty, the history of development, and the elements that lead humans to find monetary success. So much of wealth seemed to be based on circumstance. After 9/11, the basis for wealth seemed to change infinitely. Was it about money or power? I could not knock the feeling that I had to change my course to explore this question and contribute to a solution.

The more I traveled, the more I learned and saw firsthand about development challenges, and how economic infrastructure would have to change in the next millennium in order to allow the human population to thrive. I started to consider that, given my background in economics and a few years of international banking under my belt, perhaps I could add value to a field that was in need of new ideas and determined idealists. At a time when I needed a new path, and felt a pull away from my initial expectations, I slowly saw my fantasy of being a high-powered international banker no longer sustain me. My growing quest for justice and economic equality took over.

—

One of my favorite weekly columnists at the time was Thomas Friedman writing for the *New York Times*. He had a way of making sense of a completely incensed situation. He wrote about the Middle East from firsthand experience in one of his earliest books, *From Beirut to Jerusalem,* and explained in great detail the ferocity in the eyes of the Palestinians as they threw rocks, bottle caps, or pieces of glass at the Israelis to release their anger and fear. Their economic situation was miserable, yet their beliefs propelled them into a state of strength and feelings of success every time they hit an Israeli Humvee with a rock. As it related to 9/11, I started to question how religious beliefs could be so strong that someone would kill for them, even with all of the money in the world. The 9/11 terrorists were wealthy. Clearly money did not drive their passion. What made these killers feel successful?

In later books Friedman turned his focus to the growth of globalization, and how our economic future was relying increasingly on collaboration and comparative advantage. My fascination with development grew stronger. What were the mechanics of economic growth? Was it simply about the haves and have nots? Just because we are born in a developed economy, what makes our humanity any more valuable than those born in a developing nation? What makes populations (and humans) successful? Was it simply circumstance?

—

While grappling with what to do next, I read *What Should I Do With My Life?* by Po Bronson. Bronson wrote the book while going through a time of transition, recently out of work, and wondering how people seek meaning. Bronson starts the book: "We are all writing the story of our life."[5] He continues with a question: "Wouldn't it be so much easier if you got a letter in the mail when you were seventeen, signed by someone who had a direct pipeline to Ultimate Meaning, telling you exactly who you are and what your true destiny is?...and when you got confused or distracted and suddenly melted down, you'd reach for your wallet and grab the letter and read it again and go, 'Oh *right*.'"[6]

The way I see it is we have that letter, but it's not in our wallet waiting to be read. It's in our hearts and minds, waiting for stillness, quiet, and peace. That letter is the voice of our instinct, that which you can only hear when you are with yourself and your soul, and are true and honest about what you want from each day of your life. Reading this book during a time when I was questioning what I wanted for my life and career, and how circumstance would play a part, was indispensable. Bronson's stories exemplify that we are in control of outcomes from each circumstance, that decision-making is our own, that we have everything we need inside to make the greatest possible impact, despite inherent risks. I was beginning to understand the potential of humanity, and how to live a better life.

—

Trevor Waldock, CEO of Emerging Leaders, a powerful NGO that transforms the lives of disenfranchised populations in the poorest neighborhoods across the world by teaching leadership and empowerment, calls this process taking back the "life-pen." Waldock claims that everyone's life is a real story being lived out every day, the issue is "who has got the pen?", because if we don't, then someone else is writing our life story for us. For some, someone else steals the pen, perhaps in the case of a woman who has been violated or a worker who has been wronged by an employer. For others, the pen is hidden amongst anguish, sorrow, depression, or denial. Waldock teaches his students how to take back the pen, and lead their best life.

—

Waldock's personal story is one of intriguing circumstance. He was training corporate executives in the City of London around leadership development, team management, and performance measurement when he was asked to donate to a school-building program in Zambia. He had never visited Africa, so his friend running the project suggested he do so. In 2005 he flew to Lusaka and traveled into the slums outside the city to see the new school. Waldock knew immediately that the people of the slums were living in a way not suitable for humans. He was horrified by the conditions, the orphans running in the streets having lost parents to HIV/AIDS, and the obvious, extreme poverty. He realized that what this community in Lusaka lacked was hope.

He considered that, to combat decades of hopelessness, what was needed most was leadership. Since his career had been spent teaching that very skill, Waldock realized that it was these communities that needed the leadership skills, and the power to write their own stories, not the corporate executives living in downtown London.

Shortly after Trevor's visit in Zambia, he started Emerging Leaders to test his theory that world-class training could bring life-changing results to the poorest of the poor. He has held steadfast to the belief that circumstance should not determine your future. That just because someone is born into crippling poverty does not mean they cannot be given the skills and confidence to build their lives into something meaningful.

Waldock's results have been beyond comprehension, and he has singlehandedly changed thousands of lives for the better. His intuition, knowing the skills he used with high-powered executives were just as applicable with poor communities in the slums of Africa, was spot on. He accepted this truth and altered his path to change circumstance. Rather than fight the urge to ignore what he saw, and return back to his comfortable lifestyle in London, he knew that he had to embrace the reality and the potential, and build fulfillment by making a difference in so many people's lives. And his work continues.

—

For some who are blinded by money, power, or clout, that sense of circumstance or opportunity is difficult to notice. Some may look back and see openings that presented themselves like windows into possibility. Others may need to examine their lives closely, in that quiet space of their soul to find it. Some find that inkling in their faith. Others find the answer to fulfillment by listening closely, letting circumstance be the guide, making the most of bumps, bends, and turns in each path.

During my soul-searching time after 9/11, I began to question what difference I could make. I started to see a new path, one that ran perpendicular to the one I was on, that meant using my economics background to improve peoples' lives. I was unsure what exactly that meant, or how it would manifest itself, but I knew that it was in me.

Since I had been away from Chicago for a year, Dave transferred law schools, and moved back to South Carolina. He mentioned that Carolina's business school had been ranked No. 1 for international business, and it piqued my interest in graduate school. In one version of myself I was living in Vermont, getting my Ph.D. in Economics and becoming a professor. Maybe the Ph.D. was a bit overzealous, and my patience had waned too much to afford me the skills to teach. I therefore decided to pursue a masters degree in the International Economics program at the Moore School of Business at the University of South Carolina that January. I began to fantasize about living a simpler life, in a small college city with my boyfriend. I knew I would miss the energy of London, but I felt ready for a change, and wanted to settle down and recalibrate. I received my acceptance letter in March 2002 and moved out of London that May, just eight months after 9/11.

—

Although I anticipated a quieter lifestyle, and the time to focus on a science that I believed in so very deeply as the solution to our global challenges (and still do), the move was a complete culture shock. Having spent the last eight years in big cities (Chicago, then London), moving to Columbia, South Carolina, was like jumping from a bullet train to a covered wagon.

The quiet and ease of South Carolina was a welcome change, though, since I had hardly had a chance to breathe before leaving London. I thought for a moment, "Did I really just quit my high-paying, highfalutin, high-profile banking job to move to the middle of South Carolina to learn about Economics?" You bet I did. It sounded so unlike the previous me. It was not part of my initial path, and something so unpredictable.

I was reminded of this when attending a friend's wedding around the time I had just moved to South Carolina. I ran into an ex-boyfriend, whom I had not seen since Northwestern days. He told me he had been shocked to hear that I was moving to South Carolina, and had always assumed I would be living in New York running a division of Goldman Sachs. He had known my previous plan, the image I had created for myself when I was 18. He knew how badly I had wanted this life I had dreamed up, of power and money and "shiny things." He also knew I had the gumption to make it happen. That, usually whenever I said I was going to do something, I did it and never stopped to look back. To try and explain my unraveling in London, the way it felt to be operating in the shoes of someone that was unrecognizable, and to be thousands of miles apart from the love of my life, was futile. I simply shrugged my shoulders and smiled. I knew that I was on a new path of discovery, and had a goal to find fulfillment, deliver impact, and use what skills I had to make this crazy world a better place. It all sounded like a pipe dream, something you hear people talk about in commencement or motivational speeches. Those who have that calling, though, know it is not a dream. The question was how to answer it and make it real.

In the end, I loved living in Columbia. The city is a special place, full of history, and, most importantly, people with outstanding kindness. I had never experienced so much community love and support, so much welcoming and gratitude. Individuals looked out for each other and respected each other's humanity, despite very obvious racial and material differences. South Carolina is like the fighter in all of us, constantly retaliating from stereotypes, economic setbacks, and feeling forgotten. I enjoyed the quiet and laid-back lifestyle, and started to feel more present each day. I loved being in school, and appreciated the opportunity to learn from very talented and well-regarded professors.

I took a small position in the Department of Research with one of the most respected international economists in the country, and interned for a few small organizations doing simple statistical analysis and forecasting. I did well in graduate school and found myself back in the saddle of "success," feeling accomplished and fueling my ego, which was useful after so many questioned my motives for leaving London in the first place. Dave and I got engaged, and I started planning a wedding. Life was easy, quiet, happy, and peaceful. Yet I knew that my need for more challenging work, and a gnawing interest to explore the issues I had been grappling with—distribution of wealth, instances of poverty, development trajectories, effective policies for alleviating poverty, trends in income, etc—were something I could not ignore.

—

Shortly into my first year of graduate school, I decided to concentrate my studies and future thesis on these questions. My advisor assigned us William Easterly's *Elusive Quest for Growth: Economists' Adventures and Misadventures in the Tropics*, a book about why development economics had all but failed in the 1980s and 1990s, and how it could eventually succeed in the next millennium. Easterly argued that economists had not yet identified the right incentive structure to promote growth. That at the root of all development solutions is a path characterized by worth. What makes shifts in policies "worth it" to improve development? Easterly, who is a professor at New York University and inspirational thought leader among development professionals, made it seem so simple—why wouldn't aid programs work if they were designed to incentivize poor governments to adapt their systems so more money flowed to those most in need? I kept questioning whether development was as simple as determining priorities for donor dollars and shuttling money to fill gaps identified by the poor.

What Easterly explained, however, based on his direct experience working for the World Bank, was that greed, power, fraud, and other externalities (things like weather, war, or other circumstances difficult to measure) inhibited this direct flow of money, and in many cases, without the proper infrastructure and policies to manage this new funding, development would surely backfire.

Reading Easterly added an intellectual curiosity to my studies, and his theories would continue to permeate the back of my mind as I scaled the jungle gym of my economic development career after grad school.

BOTTOM LINE:

Unexpected turns can shift your goals, aspirations, and actions. Circumstances have meaning and can be your best ally as you seek personal fulfillment. Making the most out of tragedies, challenges, existential questions, or personal difficulty forces us to stay human, but can also shape a more meaningful and measurable outcome.

5

Shifting Paths

While in grad school I reviewed fundamental economic principles like supply and demand, comparative advantage, the importance of marginal cost, and so on. Propelling me through these banal courses requisite for my masters was the fire within me to pursue a career in development, something I knew was like walking a tightrope given the challenge of breaking into the field and the complexity of the work.

Anyone who has felt a strong determination to make a change in their path, despite the risks, knows that the way forward is not simple, direct, or easy. I had an instinct that my circuitous path would lead me to a place where my experiences, education, and passion to make a difference would be relevant. Yet I was fearful that, if not, all this time exploring would be a waste of time. I felt a near desperation to see my work turn into something meaningful, defined for me by addressing poverty, economic stagnation, and inequity. As it turned out, the road to impact was less traveled, and it would be 10 years before I saw the results I had expected for myself.

Looking back, I see the consequence of each stone unturned. But, at that time, as I was finishing graduate school, those elements of frustration, impatience, and disappointment that I felt when I was starting my career in banking came back to haunt me.

—

Dave and I decided to move to Washington, D.C. so Dave could pursue an Army JAG position, and I could find a role in economic development after graduation. My thesis adviser encouraged me to apply to a three-year training program for graduate students interested in leadership roles within the U.S. Government. The Presidential Management Fellow (PMF) program was well regarded by U.S. agencies as the leadership entry point for many of its top recruits. While I was not sold on working for the government after graduate school, I knew that it was a viable option for a career in development. I applied to the PMF program and was overjoyed when asked to interview. Despite a very competitive year of applicants in 2003, I was invited to attend the PMF Job Fair in Washington that fall. I met with representatives from nearly every agency: the Department of State, Department of Energy, U.S. Trade and Development Agency, even the CIA. In the end, the offers I received took me away from development and into territories that neither interested me nor aligned with my background. For example, the Internal Revenue Service offered me an entry-level auditing role, and the Department of Energy, an energy economist position. I declined both and left South Carolina without a job, something I had sworn I would not do.

I spent the first few months in Washington scanning classifieds and job websites. I attended informational interviews and researched the development landscape. Despite countless interviews, nothing materialized. I began to wonder whether my fantasy of doing my part to change the world would be a reality after all. I remember the feeling of disenchantment when my Mom suggested I get a job waitressing or serving coffee, in order to pay the bills. I wondered if my transition from successful international banker to graduate student was a poor decision, one that would take me farther away from my goal of making an impact in development. I felt defeated.

Six months into my job hunt, I saw a non-PMF opening for an International Economist position with the U.S. Department of Commerce Office of Trade Policy Analysis inside the International Trade Administration (ITA). The description read like a page out of my economics textbooks, including words like *analysis, evaluation, globalization, market access*, and *negotiations*. There was seemingly little involvement in development or poverty alleviation, but something about the position description called to me. I applied, and was asked to interview.

After meeting the team and passing a security screening, which took nearly two months, I was offered the job. The team was young, vivacious, and full of innovative thinkers, and, while I realized that the position was not what I had originally envisioned for myself, I hoped that the risk would pay off.

While most of the team within the Office of Trade Policy Analysis were traveling to Geneva to assist the U.S. Trade Representative's Office in World Trade Organization (WTO)

negotiations as part of the Doha Development Round, or flying to remote locations to negotiate bilateral trade terms with
impending trading partners, my first assignment was less sexy.
Instead, I was asked to work with a team to evaluate the sugar
subsidy in relation to the price of High Fructose Corn Syrup
(HFCS). At the time, I had no idea that the sugar lobby was
contesting a lowering of the existing subsidy, which was set to
expire and would cause challenges to sugar given how HFCS
use was growing monumentally. The U.S. Government had
long supported U.S. sugar cane growers with costly subsidies,
and since HFCS prices were significantly lower than sugar,
food and beverage companies used a lot of it. Congress gave
our analysis ample attention, as lobbyists from both sides of
the industry were knocking on representatives' doors trying
to influence policies for the future.

The "sugar study," as it became known throughout Commerce, garnered a lot of attention. It was one of the first
econometric and forecasting analyses done by our office
(which focused mostly on analyzing manufactured goods and
services trade policies). Truthfully, I did not enjoy the work,
and felt like I was constantly playing catch-up. Though I was
a trained economist, and have always been adept at number
crunching and data analysis, this work was dry and repetitive.
The analysis felt grinding, and I grew impatient with the mi-
nutiae. I wished to be in Geneva with my colleagues where
the action was. I enjoyed the debates with the representatives from the sugar and grocery lobbies, but not the data
elements of the work. The engagement with the lobbyists was
intriguing to me, though, in that their role was to serve as a
hybrid between the political leaders I worked with inside of

the government, and the corporate leaders that wanted to see a market model of supply and demand work effectively.

We finalized the study within six months, which allowed me to begin working on trade policy, something that seemed more relevant to my end goal. As it turned out, I found myself referring back to the sugar study when I began working with food companies years later as we strategized their supply chain sustainability priorities. Each step along my path helped me build a more formidable road toward finding my true impact, to becoming a change-maker.

—

Once engaged in the trade policy analysis element of my initial job description, I began supporting one of the Market Access leads, who was traveling to Geneva every couple of weeks to support the head of the U.S. Trade Representative's Manufactured Goods negotiating team. The energy and constant action was addicting. I reveled in getting calls from Geneva early in the morning and late at night, helping my colleagues who were desperate for a quick number that would go into a policy pitch either in a bilateral or multilateral negotiation setting. The work was hard, but rewarding. It became clear early on that the work of our team was critical to the success of our country's trade engagements, and that was empowering.

When the Market Access lead went on maternity leave, I was asked to fill in on her behalf. Here was my shot to travel to Geneva and support the Trade Rep's team. I felt a mix of nervous energy and adrenaline. I was completely paralyzed by the thought of making a mistake, and yet was buoyed by the confidence of my bosses and team that I could carry the weight. The first negotiating experience was everything I had expected. Late, caffeine-laced nights, last-minute edits to negotiating texts, and frantic calls back to Washington to get updated numbers for the drafting papers. I felt completely exhilarated, and, to this day, the opportunity was one of the most memorable in my professional career.

Not long after I began participating in WTO and Free Trade Agreement (FTA) negotiations, my boss came into my office and threw a fat folder on my desk. Written on top was "3Rs." She told me to review the materials and determine what the U.S. position should be. Puzzled, I began to read through the briefs and FAQs, written for the U.S. Department of State by the Government of Japan. I learned that an international effort spearheaded by Japan and supported by the United Nations Environmental Program was to identify better approaches for trade among recycled, remanufactured, and reused (the 3 "R") goods. While I had always considered myself a steward of the environment, I had never considered a career in environmental sustainability. Economic development and environmental responsibility were not mutually exclusive, but I had not considered the roles resource use and environmental trade played in improving poverty.

After reviewing all of the materials in the folder, I realized that with the 3Rs scope of work came a potential engagement in international diplomacy around issues like chemical usage, sustainable consumption and production, recycling, and trade of used goods. I recognized immediately that, if the United States was not part of this effort, it would be politically detrimental. I recommended that there should be some involvement in, or at least attention paid to, the 3Rs Initiative and suggested I act as the lead. It was risky to do so, since certainly someone at a more powerful level should hold such a diplomatic position within Commerce, but I offered myself up anyway. I was extended the opportunity to build out the policy position on behalf of Commerce, and begin regular briefings with the Assistant Secretary. I took an enormous risk volunteering to act as lead on an issue about which I knew very little. But this risk proved to be the impetus to change my career path in a way I would never have guessed as I gradually became the expert of all things sustainability, not only in my office, but also more broadly throughout ITA. This focus would stay with me for the rest of my career as I began to explore the role of sustainability as a driver in social and economic development. Eventually, I would see opportunities to build this expertise to take me further down my path to achieving impact.

The 3Rs Initiative was an amazing portfolio to manage, since along with it came once-in-a-lifetime opportunities to represent the U.S. Government in international dialogues facilitated by the United Nations, representing the view of multinational companies, and partaking in multi-agency decision-making with the Department of State, White House Council on Environmental Quality, and Environmental Protection Agency. Without question, the experience of leading the Department of Commerce stake in the 3Rs catapulted me into a new sphere of defined success, where I got to brief the Secretary, travel internationally to help develop the global 3Rs plan of action, and engage with corporate leaders. Between this level of engagement, and my work with the U.S. Trade Rep's office, what I most fantasized about before embarking on this role at Commerce, the things I thought I would achieve "someday," became a reality. I traveled around the world (on one trip I flew west to Japan for a 3Rs meeting, then to Geneva for a WTO meeting and back to DC in three weeks, legitimately circling the globe) and helped dictate policy that would have an impact on communities all over the world. I was energized by the promise of this career to effect change for communities most in need.

One of my most profound experiences was working on a medical devices text with other WTO members as part of the Doha negotiations. We were debating tariff rates for bed nets, traditionally used by developing countries to prevent mosquitos from passing on harmful diseases like malaria or yellow fever. I vividly recall the India delegation pleading to zero out tariffs for the bed nets. At the time, bed net imports into countries like India were charged an extra tariff as high as 33 percent, making the cost prohibitive for the government (or any nonprofits working in India) to purchase at the scale necessary for mass distribution. We negotiated a tariff lowering, ensuring a price high enough to retain quality production, yet low enough to encourage ample flow of the products to the communities that needed them most. It was a combined win for freer trade, for development, and for global health. The process ingrained in me the notion that these discussions were as much about humanity as they were about economics.

—

The process is never that simple, however, nor are the decisions easily made. When representing your country internationally, every word is measured, every insinuation questioned, and every comma analyzed. There is a hierarchy implicit in diplomacy. Richard Nixon, even with all of his neurosis, easily summarized some of the more quirky elements of working in politics. He once said about policy makers: "Any change is resisted because bureaucrats have a vested interest in the chaos in which they exist." What Nixon was implying was that policy makers thrive on the uncertainty of politics, and are tasked with making sense out of the chaos. They would be without direction if every decision or negotiation were straightforward. Accordingly, policy making is painstakingly slow, with each word analyzed for meaning, each constituent having to offer a lengthy position for consideration, and multiple layers of approval needed for nearly every adjustment. Given this, making policies actionable is nearly impossible. Since my urgent need to see impact did not allow for much patience, I did get frustrated after some time with such little movement despite the energy and effort we were putting into our work on trade.

—

Within the paths to finding fulfillment, whether through a career or in one's personal life, there is a lot of weaving in and out of moments of clarity, times that seem to be successful, times you think you are making an impact, and other times you feel you are falling on your face. For me, the lack of action began to feel like failure. After spending two years at

Commerce, I started to think about the corporate leaders I engaged with as part of their lobbying efforts to help inform Commerce actions, and how hard they pushed their agendas with our agency, as well as with Congress and across the government, and wondered whether stronger impact was feasible within a private sector environment. Curious, I started learning more about lobbying and the types of opportunities for those with policy backgrounds working for trade associations, corporate public affairs teams, or lobbying firms. It was 2006, and environmental sustainability was catching on. The need for policy expertise around issues like recycling, materials restrictions, energy use, design for environment, and waste was building among government and private sector actors, as corporates tried to act ahead of regulation, and the government worked to keep corporates in check. I decided to make a move to the "other side" to test out the theory that faster movement may come from the private sector, and accepted a job offer lobbying for the technology sector.

—

You know that feeling when you see a movie star in real life? How, in person, his or her features are more realistic and human, and a small percentage of that idyllic quality is lost? That feeling was a bit of how I experienced lobbying. The reality was nowhere near my fantasy. But, the experience, relationships made, and opportunities it afforded stayed with me for the rest of my career. I learned that, despite semblances of political power, people are just people. People have humanity, which transcends cultures, generations, prestige, and backgrounds. There is no denying that, while each of our challenges may be different and our struggles change, we all want to be successful, be worthy, and find fulfillment.

I had no greater feeling of gratification than when I was in the middle of an intense negotiation over language that could determine the fate of a long-contested policy, and I found a way to make a staffer, a Congressperson, or foreign diplomat smile. They (and you) become a little more human, and a little less mechanical. Finding the thing that brings the human being out of the hard shell is not easy. It takes a skill that cannot be taught. But when you find that entry point, that "in" to the other person's soul, it changes the game. The work you are doing becomes more about the human interaction and relationship forming, and less about the close of the deal. When the end product of your interaction becomes about a relationship milestone, it has more meaning, more upside, and can be more successful. When you start to see the faces around the negotiating table as those of humans with their own thoughts, feelings, and opinions, and you consider that those thoughts, feelings, and opinions shape how their decisions are made, negotiating becomes a lot easier and oftentimes better for both sides.

But after a while, the luster wears off. At least it did for me. Maybe it's the process of politicizing issues that are so critical to the future of mankind, or squabbling over nuanced language that, in the end, won't make any change to the status quo. But lobbying was certainly not my path. While I gained much insight into the world of technology and the issues that are pertinent to the sector, I also learned how to take risks by communicating difficult issues with individuals of all types, paying heed to their humanity.

During this time, I learned to look ahead, try different things, absorb knowledge from those around me, build my network, strengthen relationships, and determine what made me fulfilled and where I felt successful. By paying attention to opportunity, I was able to help build a new program linking technologists to the needs of developing economies and advance work like One Laptop Per Child, which, in 2007, was just getting off the ground providing low-cost laptops to children in impoverished, rural communities across the world. Through this effort, I became engaged with organizations like the Grameen Foundation, ONE.org, the Center for Global Development, and the Gates Foundation. I started following discussions at the World Economic Forum in Davos and the evolution of the TED Conferences. I was asked to travel to China, Japan, and Europe to understand the way international audiences were identifying the intersection of technology, sustainability, and development. It was through this period of exploration that I learned about an organization working with companies to improve sustainable development by focusing on protecting our global natural resources and its intersection with humanity. Now this, I thought, was worth exploring.

BOTTOM LINE:

The experience of changing direction and finding alternative routes to fulfillment can be rife with challenges and setbacks, difficulties, self doubt, frustration, and a wish that time would move faster. During this time you must keep going, try different things, learn from those around you, build your network, build relationships, determine where you feel success, what makes you tick, and eliminate what brings you down.

6

Ah! This is What It Feels Like

A vivid memory of one morning in South Carolina stayed with me for a while after graduate school ended. It was 2002 and the air was humid, with a touch of a breeze. It was enough of a breeze to send me to Starbucks before class for a latte, something I rarely did since I saved my coffee time for studying. While I lingered there a few minutes, biding time before my class started, I noticed some text on the back of the coffee cup. The text shared information about Starbucks' sustainable coffee sourcing program, called Coffee and Farmer Equity (C.A.F.E.) Practices. The logo associated with the program was that of an NGO that I later learned was working with Starbucks on its ethical sourcing program and climate change investments in countries where Starbucks grew its coffee. I was intrigued since I had never before thought about the process Starbucks, or any other coffee company, took to grow or roast its coffee. I certainly had never considered the role the actual farmers played. I noticed a factsheet about the program on a nearby bulletin board and read about the commitment Starbucks made to invest in programs that would ensure its farmers were paid fairly, treated well, and had no incidences of child labor or gender discrimination. The program also helped to protect the environment by ensuring limited pesticide usage, helping keep the soils healthy, and working on water quality improvements. The pairing of an NGO with a massive company like Starbucks? Intriguing. I remember thinking that it was this type of program that I should learn more about.

—

Partnerships between NGOs and companies were nearly unheard of until the early 1990s, when, after facing harsh criticism from the general public over the mounting waste caused by the fast food industry, McDonald's turned to the Environmental Defense Fund (EDF) to analyze its packaging problems and develop effective solutions. (McDonald's announced a massive overhaul to its packaging and waste program accordingly and, in addition to eliminating 300 million tons of waste, it was able to save money on the new packaging, at a tune of nearly $6 million per year.)[7] Other companies took notice, as did NGOs, and, increasingly, companies became targeted as change agents.

Into the early 2000s, corporate social responsibility (CSR), an approach of considering people, planet, and prosperity in business decisions, began to take hold. NGOs were shifting their efforts to attract new private sector partners. Companies were motivated initially by their consciences, recognizing that joining forces with an NGO would help avoid criticism from activist organizations like Greenpeace. Eventually, the motivation behind CSR shifted as companies began to see profit opportunities from programs that made energy use more efficient, operations more streamlined, factories less wasteful, and production more closely located to point of sale. Additonally, consumers became more aware of how products were made and how brands managed their CSR priorities. I did not have visibility into this trend while in graduate school, but the Starbucks program was certainly an indication that times were changing.

—

I thought about the NGO on the coffee cup when, as part of my firm's advocacy efforts, I was researching organizations partnering with the technology sector to advance development priorities. As I learned later, the NGO was ubiquitous for helping companies invest in sustainable development programs globally. I started following news and outcomes of their work, favoring their approach and methodologies as a way of shifting the mindset of corporates towards better practices, as well as consumers towards better consumption patterns.

I had become more versed in CSR over the years, specifically the link between sustainable development and economic prosperity. Certainly, making better use of our natural resources, and leveraging private sector engagements in places where companies sourced their products had the potential to grow employment, shift markets, and attract greater investment. I had begun following climate change negotiations under the auspices of the United Nations Framework Convention on Climate Change (UNFCCC) as they related to the development of carbon markets, an evolving focus of our technology stakeholders. I recognized that climate change was increasingly considered by the private sector as an operational and material risk, and thus garnered the attention of top decision makers. The NGO was beginning a new strategy to address climate change by investing in natural resource projects like forest protection, tree planting, and land restoration in partnership with companies and other donors. I could envision the challenge of managing this behemoth scope of work with corporate actors across different sectors, and the thought of doing so was energizing.

Though lobbying was not as glamorous as I had expected, I was relatively satisfied with my role, and had not planned to leave. My curiosity about working for a mission-driven organization like the NGO, however, stayed with me, and I would find myself wondering whether another career move would mean a more direct impact on communities in poverty-stricken regions. The nagging feeling that there was still more for me in my career to give back fully, to deliver benefit to humanity at a level I had not yet reached, and to trust my instinct to move forward, made me think that shifting gears, yet again, to a mission-driven organization, would lead me to the fulfillment I sought. But with another job search came a new level of frustration with myself over my inability to stay put more than two years, and wondering what was wrong with me when I got impatient by the pace of action at each organization where I worked. I started to think I was the problem, not the jobs themselves. Yet, as I thought about my legacy and my ability to make an impact, I put that aside, knowing that risking another job search was more important than the optics of it. Isn't the search for meaning what life is all about?

I noticed that the NGO was starting to hire more staff with backgrounds in policy making. I took a risk and applied for two of the job openings, wondering if my CV was fit to qualify me for consideration as the lead on the NGO's climate change strategy, the job description that most piqued my interest. After several rounds of interviews, I was offered the job. Shifting from lobbying to working for an NGO was unconventional. In D.C., most policy professionals elevate lobbying as one of the most coveted jobs. For me, I hoped that making an impact would eventually come from diverting my path towards mission-oriented work.

—

I was mostly right in my assumption, since the NGO worked with rural communities in some of the most impoverished regions of the planet. The learning curve was steep, however, since the NGO's focus was largely around natural resource conservation, and less so around economic development or policy. That said, the mission was shifting to include more focus on the link between the environment and economic improvements in poor regions of the world. I arrived at the perfect time to put my skills to use and contribute to measurable impact.

—

Over my first three years at the NGO, I felt more satiated by my day job than at any time I could recall. It was as if I had found the perfect mix of challenging work, smart colleagues, inspiring energy, and pure dedication to a mission that each one of us working there believed in wholeheartedly. I remember thinking that I would work for the NGO forever, that leadership would have to drag me out of there. I was deeply committed to the work and direction of the organization.

—

After completing our goal of developing a dynamic climate change strategy, and associating it into each of the organizational departments, I realized a need to shift my attention to an issue more resourced by the NGO, since resources (financial and human) dictated what was successful or not. I was able to transfer my focus to one of the growing drivers of climate change: agriculture. At the time, a team within the corporate relations department at the NGO was looking for someone to take on the climate and agriculture portfolio. With the overall climate change strategy process properly associated into the NGO units, I put my name in the hat. I made the move with another burst of excitment and enthusiasm for something that was challenging in its opportunity for steep learning.

As part of this new role, and in a twist of fate, nearly eight years to the date after first learning about the partnership between the NGO and Starbucks, I was asked to take over the management of the partnership. To find a position that was worthy of each kink of my path was gratifying, and despite the number of times I wondered what it was all for, I felt that the NGO was the answer. I felt like I had found my home. This was where I was meant to be. This was where I could make the most diffierence.

The irony of it all hit me the hardest while in rural Indonesia for Starbucks' annual Origin Experience, a learning trip for high-performing Starbucks partners (how Starbucks refers to their employees) to learn in greater detail about how coffee is grown, processed, milled, and eventually brought to market. I had flown halfway around the world to show Starbucks leaders how farmers in Sumatra were working toward improving their coffee quality, and building resiliency to changes in their climate. The projects we visited were funded by the company and managed by our team at the NGO.

While in Sumatra, Starbucks asked if we could work on an ancillary project, something that would allow the partners to get their hands dirty and contribute directly to one of the communities we visited. It turns out that one of the villages needed a nursery to house its coffee seedlings. Starbucks agreed to sponsor the building of the nursery, and also to help build the infrastructure while we were in town visiting. So vital was the nursery to the community's future in coffee, that the land owner, who had offered his valuable land to build the nursery, threw us an amazingly lively and festive party in appreciation. He opened his family's modest home to our group of nearly 50 people and scraped together enough money from the nearby farmers to treat us to local sweets and coffee.

The landowner played us music, and we sang and danced in celebration. The experience was unlike anything I had ever had, bringing to life all of those words on the coffee cup, and making the NGO's work with Starbucks so worthwhile in every way I could imagine. I felt such a sense of pride; pride for the dedication I had given to find myself in this place, with this company, and representing such critical work. I felt tied to the community despite the inability to utter one word of of their language. And I felt at peace that I could finally see the impact of my work in the soils of Sumatra.

—

When you work for an NGO, there is an assumption that mission is what drives you. When you lead an NGO, mission becomes akin to your life's work. The job of a CEO is to impart that feeling from within onto your staff. It is to pass on the passion and inspire consistent action. No one makes that more clear than Pierre Ferrari, CEO of Heifer International. Heifer's mission is to end world hunger and eliminate poverty. Pierre's mission is to make it happen.

I met Pierre in 2014 when I had first begun my consulting company, shortly after Heifer hired me for a short-term project. I had spoken to Pierre by phone before, and exchanged occassional emails with him, but when I first met him for breakfast at the famed Tabard Inn near Dupont Circle, I knew immediately that Pierre took his mission seriously. We jumped into a dialogue about the truth behind food insecurity, and what he and I both thought it would take to eradicate hunger. We discussed the market dynamics of big food companies and the investments many of them were making into supply chain improvements that would help solve our global food shortages. Pierre had an urgency about him, almost as if time was running out to solve our biggest problems. He had a childlike curiousity about him, too, combined with an energy that was palpable. He jumped from idea to idea with excitement and enthusiasm, prepared to try anything if only to address our crises of humanity. I thought I would be intimidated by Pierre, given his high profile among the development circle, but the opposite was true. I saw in Pierre a version of myself—someone with an instinct to get moving, to waste little time, to take risks, and to make an impact.

—

Pierre was born in the Belgian Congo (now the Democratic Republic of Congo) where growing up he was influenced by his grandmother, who ran a successful vegetable business buying from local farmers and selling to restaurants in the city. Pierre recalled how important creating this market linkage was to the farm communities outside of Elizabethville where he lived. Pierre's grandmother was helping to support the well-being and success of these farmers, who otherwise would never have an opportunity to sell in the city.

Working summer jobs as a delivery boy, Pierre happened to meet a high level executive at the regional Coca-Cola operation. Impressed with Pierre's work ethic, the executive offered Pierre a job after college conducting market research for Coke in Johannesburg, South Africa. After receiving his MBA, Pierre was given a more senior marketing role within the company. Pierre moved up the ranks, eventually becoming Chief Marketing Officer of Coca-Cola in the Americas after nearly 20 years with the business.

One of his most vivid recollections during that time was when he encouraged his oldest son to limit his soda intake because of the sugar content. Pierre's son asked innocently how he could suggest such a thing when he spent each day selling the very product he was insinuating was unhealthy for his son. Pierre was rattled by that moment, and, while he had loved his experience at Coke, he realized it was time to make a change. Having served on the marketing board of the nonprofit CARE for some time, Pierre had come to know the CEO quite well. After Pierre left Coke, and aware of the opportunity for Pierre to leverage the human spirit for the better, CARE's CEO asked Pierre to join him as Special Assistant.

While at CARE, Pierre learned about the intricacies of development, the painstaking nuance of trying to change people's lives, and the inherent patience necessary to make even the smallest mark on humanity. That experience propelled Pierre to seek even greater opportunities to make a positive impact, becoming an advocate for the most impoverished and disenfranchised populations. For a while during this time, Pierre dabbled in impact investing and joined the board of Ben & Jerry's. He was intrigued by the notion of building wealth in distressed areas, transforming social enterprises.

Now, at the helm of Heifer, Pierre has set a goal for himself and his colleagues: to effectively eliminate hunger and poverty from our awareness. A grand plan, no doubt, but one that only someone like Pierre, with a thirst for change, a commitment to deliver on his dream, and a belief in humanity, can truly affect. Pierre is not shy in saying that the legacy of Heifer is his life's work, but he does not consider it his job. It is his passion, his love. He feels lucky to work on meaty assignments to solve some of our trickiest global challenges. Pierre thrives on his insatiable curiosity and hopes to keep learning and challenging himself.

Pierre is unique in his drive to change the world. While there are millions of changemakers doing amazing work all over the world, Pierre is someone who has the special ability to use collective action and the energy he brings to address the most complex and monumental challenges of our time.

—

I felt a similar sense of purpose every time I heard the NGO's CEO speak. He had a passion for the work we were doing and an uncanny ability to craft his messaging so each one of us felt a special connection to him, his commitment, and the organization. Each time I questioned my future at the NGO, I would listen to the CEO speak and my heart would melt back into my chest, a feeling of God-like awe coming over me for the drive he had to make a difference through our work. There were many times I would feel taxed by the strenuous days, the onerous travel, the feeling there were never enough hours in the day to do everything we needed done. Yet I was propelled continually by the mission, by seeing the communities we were impacting, the people whose lives we were improving. There is nothing more humbling than giving back that time, energy, and effort to make someone else's life more worth living.

—

To grow our corporate partnerships, and thus our footprint in the developing world, we had to be great salespeople. We had to persistently share the rationale for partnering with us versus other NGOs doing similar work. Resource constraints meant that all potential engagements were on the table, and in order to deliver good, meaningful work, we also had to build relationships and focus our efforts on those organizations that could fund us into the future.

The selling did not bother me so much as the way our work sometimes shifted under the guise of a donor. Rather than sticking to our mission at all costs, we often had to adjust our attention to deliver programs that matched donor or partner needs. Yet finding the intersection between the goals of our partners and the opportunities to effect change was rewarding. It was like trying to solve one of the biggest, most challenging math problems, concocting the algorithm that would deliver a return on investment for a donor and also societal benefit for the community in which we were working. The algorithm also had to factor in the role of humanity, not just in the delivery of the project, but in what made the partnership successful and valuable both to the communities on the ground and the constituencies within the donor community.

The social interactions of my work were the most intriguing since I had to balance partner demands with delivery demands. Different personalities came through in times of stress or excitement, and I had to be prepared to manage all of them so as to protect the partnership and also the integrity of our work. Reminding myself repeatedly that we are all humans, with an instinct to make tomorrow a better day than yesterday, and the future more meaningful than the past, helped me stay true to my word that I would maintain the integrity of the work and the needs of the people we served.

BOTTOM LINE:

While seeking fulfillment, it is critical to be persistent and focused on building relationships with those who have mutual interests. Focus on what value you can bring to those doing the work that inspires you. We are all just looking for a way to make our path have meaning.

7

You Can (Not?) Have it All

As a young, idealistic, and determined woman, visions of my professional future did not always account for the complexity of motherhood. I assumed I would get married and have kids, but I was certain that my career would be a priority, too. I never questioned that I would grapple with the standard "balance" equation like most working women. Was I naive? Yes! Being completely clueless about how hard it would be to manage both a family and full-time, intense career was, in some ways, a godsend. I am not sure I would have been able to embark on either journey had I known how hard it would be for me, my husband, and our extended family. I'd like to think my kids weren't horribly affected by the struggle, since we did most everything we could to put them first. But make no mistake: The struggle, my friends, is real. Certainly those challenges we face in life are what make us stronger, but I never thought to question whether following my dreams of being a successful and impactful careerwoman could coincide with ensuring my children's and husband's dreams were met, too.

—

I learned I was pregnant with my first child a week before my final interview at the NGO. Already I was wrestling with how career fulfillment would affect my unborn child. I struggled with whether to say anything about my pregnancy, but I decided to hold the news until I got the job. That decision was something I questioned repeatedly, and I felt I had to "pay back" the act of withholding the information by proving myself to be worth the hire regardless of my "condition."

I remember working late nights on strategy documents with my boss, six months pregnant and starving, and all I could think about was making sure I did a good enough job so I wasn't seen as ineffective simply because I was pregnant. I didn't want anyone to consider me incapable of handling both a pregnancy and an intense new job.

This feeling of trying to do it all manifested itself at home, too. We moved from our townhome to our current home when I was eight months pregnant with my second child. Like many women, I wanted all of our furniture perfectly in place before the baby came so I would not have anything incomplete when the baby was born. Three weeks before I went into labor, I was assembling a cabinet at 9:30 at night, sweating, and fierce with a determination that even my husband knew was incapable of interference. Was it perfectionism that drove me to try and prove I could do it all? Was I simply stubborn? Ultimately, like most women, I had a constant need to prove I could handle being smart, powerful, a committed working woman, AND a contributing, nurturing, and reliable parent and partner. Over time I understood the notion of not being able to "have it all," but I was going to do my damndest to try. Based on the countless books on this topic, and the extensive list of blogs I have read on work-family balance, I certainly was not the first, nor would I be the last, to try and make this balance equation work for my family and me.

—

In 2012, just after my second child turned one, Anne Marie Slaughter, who at the time was a high-ranking State Department official, a well-known policy pundit, and professor at Princeton University, wrote an article titled, "Why Women Still Can't Have it All."[8] In the article, Slaughter explained that it is virtually impossible for a highly successful woman to be an effective mother, while at the same time working as a high-powered professional. Something has to give. While Slaughter was at first saluted for her honesty, and the way she depicted working women giving it their all while also saving a little something for their families (God forbid themselves), Slaughter was also criticized for leaving young women without the hope that they could truly "have it all." In other words, that they could be both a successful businesswoman, stateswoman, lawyer, doctor, or any other profession, AND be a good mother, attend all sports practices, school events, doctors' appointments, etc. The role of the spouse and the quandry of finding time for oneself are all but ignored in most of the pieces written, either in support of Slaughter's diatribe, or in retaliation.

I was lucky to have a supportive and contributing partner in Dave, and we have always co-parented and held equal responsibilities as financial providers. That said, I always felt pressure to be a superwoman—one who cooked healthy meals, had a spotless and perfectly decorated home, and could manage laundry, dishes, etc. Being able to do all of these things well was part of my definition of success, along with my career advancement. Adding kids to the mix is like taking a sledgehammer to a glass table, though. All the pieces have to fall apart at some point. There's no way to keep it all together. Something must give.

—

I wanted to be a perfect mother once I had kids, but I was never the mother that could nurse on demand, or sit through music class without wondering how many more minutes I had to act out "Ba Ba Black Sheep" or befriend other mothers at the park. I struggled with the act of "playing," beat myself up for not wanting to create puppet shows, and never ever got into Pinterest. All that said, my husband and I have devoted as much of our energy as we physically and emotionally can to ensure our children are loved, healthy, happy, and kind. We have admitted to putting ourselves on the back burner in order to be as fully present as possible for our kids as full-time working parents, but now that the kids are getting older, we can finally see the skies opening up and our full selves coming back together. The simple reality is that having a fulfilling full-time career, AND being able to give to your family, are sometimes mutually exclusive. It is near impossible to do both well all the time.

—

Having started at the NGO as a soon-to-be mommy, the responsibility of that role, while also aiming to be "high powered change-maker," weighed on me. I recognize that being Mommy is and will always be the most critical change-maker role there can be, and I do not discount that notion at all, but the constant balancing of priorities, the demands of being a young, exhausted mother while also trying to contribute meaningful work at the NGO, and the personal pressure I put on myself to do both at a high-acheiving level, took a very strong toll on my emotional and physical health. I was so relieved after reading Slaughter's article, indeed breathing a huge sigh of relief (and frankly shedding many a tear) that I was not alone in this ongoing battle within myself to find that balance (and realizing that balance is almost unachievable).

Some days I would have it all together, able to put in a full day at the NGO, contribute meaningfully, think deeply, and pick up my two boys at daycare at a reasonable hour so I could enjoy some time after school with them before Dave got home and the evening began. But most days were a mix of me rushing to make it to daycare so the boys weren't the last ones to be picked up as I shot off a top-of-mind email to a corporate partner, realizing I left out a very crucial element around a proposal deadline, or rushing out the door in the morning to get the kids to daycare in time to make an early meeting, spilling formula on my suit, and forgetting my laptop at home.

Most working parents know these moments. In those moments you question why the heck you are killing yourselves each day. But then there were the moments when I would sit in a partnership meeting, inspired by the rich dialogue, confident that this partnership would be the one to end the long-standing lack of investment in a nearly forsaken part of the world where we would most certainly be making a substantive difference in many peoples' lives, and those moments silenced the doubt.

I would also have those moments of clarity, peace, and happiness with my children too; those moments when they first learn to walk, when they first smile into your eyes, when they learn to hug you and say, "I love you." As my kids get older, those moments expand in meaning as they learn to talk about their feelings, what makes them happy, what makes the day "the best—or hardest—day ever." The weight of my role as Mommy takes on an even more serious tone when shaping the future of these two souls means they can take on the challenges the world faces along with me.

—

Those early years when my children were young admittedly were incredibly difficult for me, as they are for many parents. Sheer exhaustion can be debilitating. The constant need to be physically and emotionally present is unwavering. Going to the office on a Monday morning was like stepping away for a brief vacation. I could enjoy a hot cup of coffee, read emails from intelligent people, and think creatively without interruption. It felt almost selfish to be at the office working for eight hours a day because I enjoyed it so much. Thankfully, my children were well taken care of by wonderful providers and we were lucky to be able to afford that luxury. Rushing out the door every day at 4 p.m., though, was never easy, and I often yearned to stay and partake in brainstorming or strategy discussions with my colleagues. Jumping back into email in the evenings was a must so I didn't feel any FOMO (Fear of Missing Out) from discussions that took place after I left the office each day.

While I allowed myself to grow more confident in that routine, particularly as my kids grew older and more independent, there were many moments when that confidence was called into question. It's those experiences that make being a working mother very difficult. I recall one irrational comment made to me by a senior executive at the NGO. This executive was older and male, and in my opinion lacked a very important sensitivity chip needed to work in development (frankly that sensitivity chip is needed regardless, but even more so in that line of work).

I was preparing for a trip to Indonesia, one that would take me away from my family for nearly two weeks. Of course, I was not thrilled to leave my family for so long, but I knew they would be fine, and we had a routine that went along with my traveling, something that was very important to me personally and professionally. I could never do my job well if I didn't have the ability to travel internationally, since I was working on programs that aided rural communities in impoverished nations. Traveling overseas was as much a part of my success in delivering effective impact as it was about me understanding more of the world.

In this particular instance, I was packing up my computer and putting some file folders into my bag to take with me on my trip. The executive sauntered into my office and asked me if I was ready for my trip. I told him I was and that I was excited and anxious to get going. He then proceeded to ask me how I could possibly go so far away, leave my children, leave my husband without prepared dinners, and feel good about doing so. He wondered who would take care of my children. I looked at him with an incredulity. Was he kidding? He laughed a bit, so perhaps he was. Didn't matter. I did not laugh at all. I looked him in the eye and I said nonchalantly: "My husband will take care of his children, my children, and my husband will be able to prepare dinners for himself and the children, and they will be fine. And how do I go so far away? I pack my suitcase, walk onto the plane, and I fly there. That's how."

Did I take it too far? Was I being overly sensitive? Maybe. But was he being sexist and misogynistic? Absolutely. Had he ever asked any of my male colleagues with children how they could possibly leave their wives and children and fly to Indonesia? Unlikely.

I hear the executive's voice still as I prepare for a long or arduous trip away from my family. "How could you?" I hear. And each time I tell myself that my work has meaning for me as a woman, as a mother, and as an impact maker. I am someone who seeks to change things for the better and am committed to my work because of the outcomes I know it can bring our planet—changes that are bigger than me, bigger than my family, and bigger than all of us combined. I am also committed to staying true to the promise I made to myself long ago, that I would find fulfillment and do what I can to effect change among those communities that cannot do so on their own. Some may see it as selfish—the traveling, the hours away from my kids—but I see it as the opposite. As soon as I became a mother to two gorgeous boys, I promised that I would do everything I could to teach them kindness, how to have an open heart, and to recognize that we all must do our part to change the world.

—

My ongoing struggle with finding the balance between my work and my family has not ceased, even as my children have aged. Now that they're six and eight, I can more easily explain why I may be leaving them to visit a faraway country, and why it is so important that Mommy help a company learn how to be a better company so the people that depend on that company for their income can be better off. But the challenge of balance is still present every day. I still rush to make pick up on time, and to get the boys to hockey practice, and to make a healthy dinner for the family, and to do laundry, and keep the house clean like every other parent. My husband is still incredibly supportive, and we share duties and responsibilites as equally as we can.

The struggles that we face to be good parents, partners to our spouses, daughters, friends, sisters, etc. are universal, regardless of what role we play in a profession. Ignoring the naysayers and continuing to move forward are critical, though, as long as you want to find that fulfillment. It's okay to be selfish sometimes (not all the time)! You may struggle with that balance forever, or just for a short time, but you are not alone and certainly no coworker or boss or executive has the right to tell you (whether you are male or female) how to manage the decisions you make.

Finding your path to impact is going to be met with bumps in the road and twists and turns no matter what direction you go. If you remain committed, you will find what drives you. Once you have that satisfaction, your children and the other important people in your life will thank you for teaching them, and sharing with them the lesson of staying true to your inner mission.

—

For me, I knew that working for the NGO during the time when my kids were very young was the best opportunity for me to make a difference, and yet still have stability. I was managing meaty projects, working with intelligent and challenging people, and could see myself incrementally making an impact in each of the deliverables I had. I knew that I would continue at the NGO as long as I could keep working in a meaningful way, and until I stopped being proud of the work I was doing. There were certainly times when I admired women who seemed to have more engaging work, and even those with children who seemed to have it all together enough to acheive the balance I struggled with. But I stayed where I was, shifting roles a couple of times, and finding a way to be professionally fulfulled while being as present as possible for my family.

—

As a disclaimer, I feel it important to add one point that often goes unsaid. Even when I am "present" for my kids, I do find my brain wandering, my patience waning, and my status quo needing to be challenged. I have prided myself on loving the work I do, and the commitments I have made to working on impactful projects. In some ways I could "work" way more hours in the day than most people, because to me work is not "work." It's a passion. It's a love. I have always sought work that was meaningful and impactful, and, because of that positive energy I feel when I work, I can revel in it. That is nearly impossible to turn off, even when I am with my kids. I have to be very cognizant of that pull, and to be present with my kids means forcing my brain to ignore a very strong element within me. Having children has forced me to take these breaks, however. It has been a healthy and important component of my personal and professional growth. It means I seek work that is worthy of my time away from them, and even during the time I spend working while I am with them (which we are all guilty of). I hope that, by sharing my work experiences with my kids over the years, they will grow to understand that I made good on my commitment to help those who could not help themselves, and that I did so in a way that was both personally and professionally fulfilling.

BOTTOM LINE:

It may be unrealistic to assume that balancing personal demands, obligations, interests, and the needs of your family will be unrelated to how you seek fulfillment and deliver impact. Stay true to your mission, and hold onto the hope that you will find the way through. You may have to make tough choices, but keep focusing on what drives you, ignoring the naysayers and continually moving forward.

8

Risk Before Impact

It was Albert Einstein who said that the definition of insanity is doing the same thing over and over again, and expecting different results. Working for an NGO, based on my experience and those I know who have worked (or are working currently) in that space, is incredibly rewarding on the one hand. Finding a cause you believe in so fervently that you want to spend your entire career fighting for that cause, and encouraging others to do so along with you, is admirable and inspiring.

On the other hand, it cannot be overstated how dedicated you must be to that cause to stick it out through some of the challenges that come with working within an NGO environment. Many of those challenges creep up on you in different ways, over and over again, and can drive someone with a sense of purpose to start to doubt the power of the work that brought them there in the first place.

Like Einstein's quote, I found myself trying to manage through days of uncertainty at the NGO the same way—over and over, expecting different results. I was never uncertain of the mission, or the capabilities of my colleagues to deliver; I just started to doubt the true level of impact we were having when I encountered bout after bout of risk aversion.

—

After my fifth year at the NGO, I had rotated through five different bosses and was involved in three different strategy-setting processes. To most NGO workers, this is standard practice. With funding coming in and out, donor demands changing on a dime, and leadership decision-making so rooted in what drives funding, things like strategies, job functions, and team rosters change frequently.

I started to question whether my investment in the NGO's mission was actually yielding the impact I wanted to see. With two small children now in the mix, this creeping period of doubt about the time I spent massaging our corporate partnerships to bring in additional funding for field projects that were not as robust as I would have liked to see, made me start to ponder my future at the NGO. I began to feel an impatience unlike that from the past. It wasn't about a lack of challenging work, or intellectual dialogue, or even a sense of mission. Instead, I started to question whether, as a general rule, the NGO was taking big enough risks to deliver a robust return on investment for the millions of dollars we were bringing in from corporate and other donors.

I found myself questioning authority over decision-making, and wondering if the NGO was well-positioned to innovate and advance among a fiercely competitive landscape. I would then get down on myself, realizing that even with all of the doubt in the world, I was in no position to change the direction of leadership decisions. That, in itself, brought with it a sense of hopelessness that true impact may be more far-reaching than I had even considered.

—

I recall one particular moment when I suggested we contact a new potential corporate partner, feeding off of a lead I had initiated. One of our Senior Directors said that we may want to rethink taking the risk of reaching out to this company since we had tried to do so before and it didn't go well. This made little sense to me. Isn't there a statute of limitation that expires after a certain period of time, when learning that a partnership could be beneficial, and the past can be put behind us? After all, the elapsed period of time had been nearly 10 years. I was very surprised that my colleague was suggesting we pass on the chance of a potential partnership with this influential company, one we had an entre into with room to grow.

That was just one example of a lack of vision in one regard, and a limitation among some of the leadership to try something different. I started to feel an internal struggle around the notion that so much was needed in the communities where we worked, and there was so much opportunity to address those needs through corporate partnerships, but the direction and vision from senior leadership was just not there. In addition to a sense that the impact we "could" be making with the partnerships we had was too insignificant,

I started to doubt so much of decision-making to the point where, some days, the way decisions were made seemed almost fraudulent. That we could have been more honest with our partners, and redirect resources in a direction that was more strategic or impactful, was very hard to swallow, especially since I put aside the more unconscionable days when I left banking years ago.

—

I made the difficult decision to look for (yet another) new job after several mis-attempts to address these challenges. I was hesitant to go down the road again, hoping to avoid the carousel of resume writing, interviews, and networking. Yet I felt my clock was ticking to take bigger risks, work more efficiently, and make the impact of my time away from my family more profound. I still had not found that end game for myself, where I could safely say that I was doing everything I could to effect change. I was hamstrung by thwarted attempts to keep me inspired.

I had a few uninteresting interviews, causing me to lose hope, when I learned of an opening at One Acre Fund, an amazingly innovative and successful social entrepreneurial organization helping small farmers in Eastern Africa grow more productive and successful crops.

One Acre Fund was started by a Northwestern business school graduate (hail to my alma mater!) named Andrew Youn, who, when traveling through Kenya during business school, met farmers who were unable to maintain a decent level of productivity on their farms due to lack of fertilizer, capital, and tools. These farmers were struggling to feed their families, a challenge millions of farmers grapple with every year as they wait for harvest season to sell their goods, and Andrew realized that simple changes to their business model, plus training and support, made the difference between farmers in poverty and those who were thriving. He wrote a business plan and pitched it to a few business school friends, found some funding, and moved to northwestern Kenya to test his theory.

Within the first five years, One Acre Fund had helped more than 200,000 farm families thrive with its toolbox of services and community programs. Their goal is to reach one million families by 2020, a goal they are well on their way to reaching.

I saw a posting for a Business Development Director opening at One Acre Fund in June 2013 and applied at a whim. It turns out the U.S. Director and I had crossed paths once or twice at Northwestern, so I reached out to him via some mutual friends. He was cordial and open to having a conversation. We shared ideas around the future of philanthropy and poverty alleviation, and had similar approaches to partnership. It was natural to engage with him and I was excited by the idea of working with him and his team.

After reading Roger Thurow's *The Last Hunger Season: A Year in an African Farm Community on the Brink of Change,* a book largely about the opportunities to address seasonal hunger in farming communities in Africa, focusing on One Acre Fund community families as the protagonists, I began to feel an urgent sense that this organization was where I belonged. I was drawn to the mission of helping impoverished farming communities build stronger futures for themselves, and the market-driven approach to do so. I was intrigued by Andrew Youn and his dedication to his mission, giving up nearly everything to move to Bungoma, Kenya and give all his energy to making One Acre Fund an effective and scalable program to address poverty. I was amazed by the success and viability of the model for reducing and, in many cases, eliminating hunger from the realities of One Acre Fund farm families.

As I moved further into the interview process, I was asked to fly to Bungoma and meet with Andrew as a final step in determining whether I was the right fit. I had been told that Andrew was particular about the people he hired, and wanted only the most creative, determined, and focused minds working for him. The challenges that One Acre Fund families meet every day make them deserving of the finest minds coming together to find solutions. I agreed to make the trip.

The last week of September 2013, I flew from Washington to Dubai, Dubai to Nairobi, and Nairobi to Bungoma. I was picked up in the late evening hours, dark as can be, and taken to the One Acre Fund compound. Settled into a small one-room guest house, I managed to fall asleep to the sound of birds chirping and dogs barking. When I awoke, I joined the staff at the center part of the compound for breakfast and coffee. The air was cool and fresh, the grass so green it looked almost blue, and the sky as clear as I have seen.

I was taken to meet with several farm families, to experience a farm training, to visit one of the seed nurseries, and to the Bungoma offices to meet with several staff that didn't live on the compound. Bungoma itself was bustling with locals selling fruits, vegetables, crafts, clothing, and household wares. The roads were dusty and well-traveled, and the people worn with hard work but smiling all the same.

The farm families I met were living in one-bedroom shacks, often eight or nine people per home, yet were so proud of their crops and also thankful for their opportunity to work with One Acre Fund. You could see how pivotal the organization had been, and would continue to be, for these families. I was humbled and in awe of the spirit of the families, and could see the yearning for knowledge. Being in Kenya made me desperate to get to work helping these and other similar families who so clearly had the ambition, the drive, and the fight to make life better. But they needed new skills, the support of their community, and the model of One Acre Fund to do so.

I enjoyed a lively dinner conversation with several more staffers that evening, and headed back to my guest house to work on my presentation for Andrew the following day. It was comforting to hear the team laughing and enjoying themselves well into the evening as I slowly drifted to sleep.

The following day I gave my final interview presentation to Andrew, packed up, and said my goodbyes to the staff. It was pouring rain and I wondered how we would take off from Bungoma, the body of the plane shaking with wind. The one-hour plane ride back to Nairobi was treacherous, but, not unlike the plight of the farmers I met, the plane fought its way back to stability. Back to Nairobi, then Doha and ultimately to Washington, my two days away and nearly four additional days of travel brought me home where I could absorb the experience.

—

I found out two days later that I did not get the job. It turns out that, after my final presentation, Andrew decided to re-think the position all together, rewrite the job description, and consider a different skillset. Fair to say, I was heartbroken. I had imagined a career with One Acre Fund being my ticket to finding true impact around an issue that was, in my mind, one of the most fundamental challenges we have as a global society—feeding those that cannot find the most efficient ways to feed themselves. Finally, I would find my true path to impact. But no. It was risky of me to get attached to the idea of supporting One Acre Fund, but I was in need of such risks. I was grasping for work that would test innovative solutions to the most sticky problems. Yet this would not be my path.

—

I could not shake the notion that getting closer to the development needs of our planet was what motivated me, and had been the case since I left banking and went back to school to study the essence of what makes development successful or not. Once you see such poverty, it is impossible to imagine spending your time working on anything else. The need is so vast and the extent so great in many parts of the world completely untouched by American interests.

In the years since my visit to Kenya, I have seen some of the poorest communities in the world, and I still think about the families in Bungoma and how hard they were fighting to improve their status quo. I also continue to share the story of One Acre Fund, given their success in changing the shape of poverty across Africa.

—

Taking risks is not always about doing something out of the ordinary or unexpected. In some cases, taking risks is about learning to change something within yourself that has plagued the way you make choices in your personal life or your career. My cousin, Rachel, said something to me recently that struck a chord. She said, "*People who demand the very best are the ones who get the very best.*" In a world full of constant change, when confidences can be easily broken, it is important to remember that the energy we put out is equal to what we take in. If we seek the best for ourselves, and know that we deserve to be treated well, respected, and listened to, then that is exactly how we will be treated. Yet, if we feel we are not enough, that our words don't matter, our thinking is irrelevant, or our ideas are silly, that is how others will treat us. Taking hold of our future makes us demand a better one.

Lorna Davis, the CEO of DanoneWave, proves this theory. Lorna has spent her career working in the food sector, living all over the world and advancing to positions of power along the way. Born in South Africa, Lorna had few expectations for herself as a professional after university. She certainly never envisioned a life in business, as she studied sociology and anthropolgy. She had a fascination with the psychology of factory workers, and with apartheid so vividly present in her upbringing, she assumed she would use her anthropology skills to improve the state of ordinary people.

Stumbling into a marketing position at Unilever, which was recruiting on her campus, she spent the next 15 years moving up the ladder, relocating to Australia and taking over as marketing director of a snackfood business. With no real dreams or aspirations aside from making more money and taking on more responsibility, Lorna found herself saying "yes" to anything that came her way. She never questioned authority, or doubted that moving "up" and becoming more powerful was the best approach to her path. She worked hard, paid her dues, and eventually became President of Kraft Foods in China by the time she reached her late forties.

After six years in China, Lorna was tired of the race. Yet again she was promoted by her company and moved to the United States. She realized she had spent her whole career saying "yes" and wanted to start saying "no." With an even more powerful and higher-paying role waiting for her, however, Lorna was stuck. She was unhappy, unfulfilled, and felt miserable most days, finding tears filling her eyes each morning in anticipation of the day before her. Despite how unhappy she felt, she continued to struggle with finding her authenticity, and could not find a way say "no" within the path before her, to find change that would make her feel more fulfilled, and, most importantly, that would help her uncover her true self.

But then something started to happen. Each morning Lorna peered out her windows overlooking Central Park, wondering how she would get through each day. She started to take walks in the park and once met a man named Armando sleeping on a park bench. Armando was a recovering drug addict. In getting to know Armando, Lorna learned that while he had been an "olympic addict," able to defeat and outsmart anyone who tried to stop him in his drug use, he finally had a moment of grace when everything changed and he realized that seeking approval, power, status, and money was his downfall. His story resonated since Lorna, in her own way, was trapped in a similar cycle. Armando had realized that being present, being honest, and taking the risk to say "no" would save his life. Befriending Armando helped Lorna see the same.

Armando remains one of Lorna's closest friends, and to her great surprise, it took a deep and honest friendship with a homeless man to uncover what had been keeping her from finding her inner "no" for so many years. Simply opening herself up to the possibility and opportunity of learning that power and money do not provide all the answers helped Lorna find what she calls the "pilot light" inside as she seeks meaning in the journey of life. She learned to start trusting herself, to listen to her inner "no" and not say yes to everything. She learned to fight for what she believes in and find a mission for the work she is so fortunate to do.

For Lorna, fulfillment is about finding a way to use the skills she's acquired in positions of power and status over the years for good. She sees her role as a business executive as the best possible place for her to deliver benefit to society by ensuring decisions are made to positively impact our planet. She calls it "bringing love to corporate America." Lorna has always maintained a level of curiosity that has propelled her into positions of power and influence. She was never satisfied with the status quo. She always yearned for more. Now her journey continues with risk, but peppered with a truth about fear, vulnerability, and transparency that she does not have the answers and can only deliver what she has learned with grace and humility. When she was younger, Lorna was always trying to prove herself. When she found her inner "no" and realized that all along she could deliver love to her work, she had truly found herself.

BOTTOM LINE:

Risk taking is different for everyone. Yet, by taking risks and stepping outside of your comfort zone, you can effect change and make significant impact. Without taking risks or confronting fears of failure, vulnerability, or seeing your true self, your potential impact is thwarted and fulfillment is squandered. Expect for yourself only the best, and that is what you will get. Your own expectations will help you set your path and determine the way forward.

9

The Day I Broke

I had returned to Sumatra in the summer of 2013 with a different group of Starbucks partners to put the finishing touches on the coffee seedling nursery we had begun the year before. The continuity felt right, and I was grateful to continue our work with the community that had become familiar. It was also incredibly rewarding to give back to families that were so appreciative, hard working, and gracious. The experience was again nothing short of oustanding, and I was thrilled to share the trip with another set of Starbucks leaders who I knew would return to Seattle with these families in their minds as they continued to improve the footprint of the coffee business.

Shortly after I returned from that trip, our team was forced to face the harsh reality that dwindling funding would not allow us to continue our work in Indonesia—we would not be able to support the community where we had built the nursery. It felt like a complete failure to me, even though I knew we would still be helping many other communities in need of assistance and whose livelihoods depended on our technical support. While that made sense to me in theory, after having established a relationship with the community in Sumatra, and building a future together in concert, I could only focus on how my long-term goal of helping impoverished communities like the one in Indonesia started to feel ephemeral. The inability to secure future funding for the work we had only begun was devastating, and it hit me more personally than it should have. Development, again, was failing the communities most in need.

Since that time, I have learned that development projects cannot, nor should not, sustain communities like the one in Sumatra. An injection of funding or infrastructure or technical expertise is critical, but from there, governments and other decision makers, leaders, and community participants must take hold and manage investments for future growth. It is nearly impossible for a private sector company, even one sourcing from the region, to singlehandedly keep a community thriving. Communities in need of assistance, whether social, economic, or environmental, will benefit from the support of a funded program, but the long-term viability of each program is dependent on the community taking responsibility to maintain, grow, and advance the work initiated by a funded project.

At the time, I understood this concept intellectually, but I was so hamstrung by the feeling that my success was tied to the funding, I could not separate that sense of empowerment from what would make the communities truly better off. It was not until I was much further removed from my time at the NGO that I could understand this, and work with donors, companies, and other partners to design programs that make this longevity an integral element.

Traveling with One Acre Fund also helped me understand this concept in a more pivotal way, and led me to question whether I was designed for NGO work after all. Although I had made a commitment to myself after graduate school to deliver impact at all costs, and give back to my fullest potential, I began to allow myself the room to think more clearly about what this really meant. Could I handle the reality of NGO work where funding is not infinite, and some communities will go bereft? Could I accept the statute of limitations on funded projects guided by donors with singular interests and the fact that not all needs can be met?

Once you travel to the field and see for yourself what poverty looks like in its horror, it is virtually impossible to give up on finding the resources to make the programs long-lasting and effective. The benefit of the type of Origin Trip led by Starbucks is that their leaders can see that reality for themselves, too. In fact, Starbucks managed to return to the Sumatra community in later years to continue supporting the nursery and the families around it. In hearing that news, I was beyond grateful for their continuity and their commitment to finish what they started.

—

I spent the early part of the Fall of 2013 on a series of proposals to donors that did not include the Indonesia work. We had identified opportunities with new corporate partners, and I was happy to focus on the new pathways. I held onto a hope that the Indonesia work would come back to us eventually. I was busy, though, and focused on the future of our program.

It is much easier to not dwell on what's missing if my life is busy. The fall is my favorite time of year as well, and, while most people make their New Years resolutions in January, I make mine in the fall. The season bears such a sense of renewal (school underway, fruit harvest, and for us Jews, the Jewish New Year of Rosh Hashanah) and commitment (hunkering down after a summer hiatus) that it is nearly impossible to start each fall without considering what the next year will bring.

Shortly after my return from Africa, I had that usual feeling of a fresh start, and found myself much more open to possibility for my future career path than ever before. I continued to balance that excitement and energy with a feeling of disappointment that the One Acre Fund opportunity did not pan out. I would share my doubt about my future with the NGO with friends and family, and admit to my level of uncertainty whether I could truly deliver the type of impact I wanted to see by working for any NGO. I wondered what a new start would even look like for me. At that point, I was feeling jaded by the lack of movement I was seeing by most NGOs, and saw One Acre Fund as one of few exceptions. I was simultaneously questioning myself, wondering if I would ever really find what I was looking for.

But what was that, exactly? If I had not found that sense of fulfillment by now, would I ever? Maybe I was being naive in assuming there was some beacon on the hill that shone a light down on me alerting me to the fact that I have "Finally

Delivered Impact!" Maybe the problem was me. I started to doubt myself continually, thinking I would never be satisfied, feeling fickle for seeking too many different types of roles, in different capacities, and making it difficult for supervisors to keep me feeling challenged and engaged. I wondered if there was ever a situation where I could feel satiated, or if I would continually blame everyone else around me for my feelings of inadequacy. I started to think deeply about exactly who I wanted to be, how I engaged with others in my organization, whether I could handle continuing down a path where I disagreed with decisions or approaches, or where so much depended on finding the right funding.

My experiences from high school, challenging my superiors who thought my writing needed work, or my grammar needed improvement, were coming back to haunt me as I felt the blood boiling in my body every time I disagreed with an approach my supervisors took or a move that leadership made around strategy. Perhaps it was time for more self-reflection. Maybe I needed professional help to deal with my constant impatience and lack of fulfillment. I kept hearing a voice deep down, though, that brought with it an unwavering confidence that I did have a knack for making development more effective. I simply could not find the space or commitment to test my approaches. I was either rebuffed or my ideas did not fit within the current strategy. In many cases my ideas were considered misaligned with the interests of our donors or partners. It was like I was handcuffed to monotony. There seemed little room for creativity, innovation, or risk.

—

About a month after returning from Africa, the bow began to break for me and my future with the NGO. I was in the Northeast, having been asked to participate in a sustainability strategy session with a large corporate partner of ours. I would join a host of other "experts" to share insights and recommendations with the corporate leadership team, and help the company craft its long-term sustainability goals.

Prior to the opening dinner session, I took some time to walk along the downtown lake, reveling in the fall beauty and utter stillness across the body of water. Downtown was quiet, with most residents having made the exodus back to the suburbs, and the silence was welcome. Being away from the office was glorious. I could feel the anger that had been burning a hole in my heart start to dissipate. I felt the room and space to think clearly—something I badly needed.

In addition to the company that had brought me to this beautiful town, there were several other big-name companies that had their headquarters there, many of which had offices situated around the lake. As I walked the loop, and saw each of the corporate logos pass me by, I started to feel a yearning to be a part of the energy that I assumed exuded from each of those companies. These were companies with missions I respected, and with programs around sustainability and impact that I deemed worthy.

In my time working with companies that made commitments to sustainable action, I always thought that sustainability and social impact could be more successful if these companies thought about their investments just a bit differently. What was needed was not just the right program or project, but the right people within the company to believe in the focus of the program, to invest time and resources, and to deliver on commitments. As I was walking around the lake I began to think about whether effective development was really about the WHO and not so much the WHAT. I had theorized in the past the concept that relationship building, making the right connections, and having the right people at the table (including and, most importantly, the program recipients) was really at the heart of effective impact delivery. That, in some cases, the beauracratic and technically focused programming we designed at the NGO took less into consideration the role of the people themselves, and more into account how the program meets certain goal requirements or objectives.

I wondered what big thinking was going on inside each building as I passed by, and visualized walking into one of those offices and finally saying all of the things I would often think when in meetings with corporate leaders, but was never "allowed" to because we had certain messages we had to deliver to close the deal. I wondered what it would feel like to make decisions based on potential impact and measures of success, to search for the leaders who were impassioned and commited to effecting change, to work on programs that were more than just the funding that came along with them.

There had been times in the past few months that friends and family members would hear me spout off ideas I had about how the NGO could function differently, or how corporates I was working with could think more collaboratively with partners. I started hearing suggestions that I leave the NGO to start my own consultancy. The rationale was that working for myself may be the only solution to the years of struggle to find the right approach to impact, let alone the fulfillment I was continually seeking. My father-in-law, in particular, suggested this idea to me repeatedly, but I always shrugged off the idea as unacheivable and downright irresponsible. How would I help support our family? How would I find work? It just was not in the cards. But as I was reveling in the peaceful meditation that crisp fall day in New England, my skin began to crawl with excitement as I thought about the autonomy that being in this city on my own, with my own opinions, and program suggestions and solutions to big challenges, could present.

That energy stayed with me the next day during our strategy session. I was surrounded by some of the best thinkers in sustainability, brainstorming solutions to this company's really tough, seemingly unbeatable challenges. We were addressed by the CEO, who unabashedly implored us to put our humility aside and think innovatively, be risky, and deliver on the passion that brought us there that day. My contributions to the dialogue were provocative, yet met well. I could sense that my input was useful, my opinions mattered. My yearning to challenge this company to deliver real impact was obvious. In some ways I was taking a risk by sharing my personal opinions and being honest about what this company could do differently. I veered from my talking points, since they were old hat to this company and did not offer much in the way of new thinking. Instead I shared points based on MY knowledge and experience, and not that of the NGO. I felt that the energy from my ideas was unmatched, and what was clear was that I was in that room for who I was and what I brought, not because of the organization I represented. Added to the mix was the fact that this relationship was one I re-introduced to the NGO based on networking I led on my own, and this company brought me to this strategy session because of my input and potential to deliver change, not the NGO's.

Like a lightening bolt it hit me that for the first time, I did not equal my organization or my boss or their logo or their approach to management. I was ME and was able to provide value based on my worth. This engagement was just what I needed to reignite my confidence and help me realize that the problem I was facing at the NGO was not just about me and my inability to find a satisfying role for myself. It was just as much about the environment, and my clear need to be less shackled to the hierarchy and structure I had around me at the time. I needed to find that trust in myself and my thinking again. It felt liberating to exert my strengths and showcase that I *did* know what I was talking about, I COULD be an expert. Validation still clearly mattered to me. I needed it at that moment.

—

Over the course of the two-and-a-half days I spent with the sustainability advisory group and the corporate leaders of this company, I grew less shy in providing advice based on my expertise that I knew could lead to actual change. It was liberating to free myself from the confines of only speaking to what could drive funding opportunities. My opinions mattered, and it was clear the company could feel my drive to deliver impact.

In conversations with several other participants, I noticed that a few were consultants in the room. They had joined the session as experts in their fields, to provide input, give suggestions and speak their minds based on their knowledge base. There were few limitations on the extent to which they participated and shared information. I admired their situation and, in many ways, wished I was in their shoes.

—

Between the time I spent in near-meditation by the lake when I first arrived, and the discussions I had with the advisory committee members, I felt increasingly inspired. Sitting in my hotel on the final night of my visit, I began to sketch out what types of interventions between NGOs and companies made sense to me, how impact could be more easily delivered. I began to research consulting companies and sole proprietorships to determine what others were doing in this space, and I jotted down some notes that could, in some alternate pipe dream universe, turn into a business plan. The seed had been planted.

—

I returned to Washington to jump back into a deeply involved proposal development process that had been ongoing for months. A lot was riding on the success of this proposal, including the potential future relationship with the corporate partner involved. The pressure to deliver innovative thinking to the partner, and bring in substantive funding for the

NGO, was intense. I took much of it on myself, sensing that if the proposal process went less than smoothly, it was on me.

My boss' boss and I had a volatile relationship and while, in some ways, I thought he liked and respected me for my work, in others I suspected he saw me as a tool to help propel him within the organization. I simply did not trust him. Trust, it so happens, is critical in a work relationship as in any relationship. He was relatively new to the NGO, and had claimed he had taken the position to avoid retirement and "give back." He often reminded us that he was not in it for the money, having spent most of his career working for big, shiny consulting companies. He wanted to "fix" us, he would say.

Field visits with the boss' boss were necessary, as he needed to see the type of work we were supporting. I recall one visit to Southern Mexico when we were having dinner the night before our farmer visit, and the boss' boss snapped at the waitress in the hotel restaurant for bringing wine that he thought was subpar. I was absolutely mortified. I was not raised to treat anyone like that, especially in a community we were visiting to help. Development work is NOT EASY. The field teams that help run the programs are the heros of development, not those of us who find the money to keep them going. I always believed that those on the ground deserved the most respect out of anyone at the NGO. I think deep down he felt that way too, and did want to see greater good come from his work. I appreciate that, at the time, we did need some hand holding, but his approach wasn't working.

Our team environment around this time was simply unhealthy and borderline toxic. Many of my colleagues chose to leave, and it felt as though this proposal was all I had to keep me focused on my end goal of simply doing good work.

—

A week after returning from my epiphany-filled trip to New England, the boss' boss and I were preparing a presentation to the big corporate partner on the elements of our proposal. With all of the back and forth between the experts at the NGO and the decision-makers at the corporate partner, our proposal had been whittled down a bit, and I was feeling somewhat gloomy about the prospects for the partnership. I still had hope, though, that the work both sides agreed to would be influential and substantive enough to carry the partnership forward, eventually finding ways to scale. With the months of negotiating behind us, we had found common ground with the corporate partner. I would struggle with the potential for impact that we left on the cutting room floor after the process was all said and done, but I was emotionally exhausted by the energy from the back and forth. We managed to make progress and keep our relationship intact.

—

Then came the day I broke.

—

Working from home so I could attend a program at my son's school, I was emailing back and forth with the boss' boss as we worked to revise the presentation. I felt torn between trying to get everything perfect, and making it to my son's school on time. We had until the end of the day to finalize all materials, and I mentioned to my boss' boss that I had a time deadline after which I would no longer be able to focus on this presentation. The proposal was in great shape, so I suspected we would need no new changes. I received another email about 10 minutes before I was to leave for my son's school with very nasty and demeaning language about how little effort I was putting into this work, how careless I was, and hinting at incompetency. Then came the criticism over the agenda when he hung up on me...I was not sure which made me the most angry, but I was mad.

—

For a reason I still cannot explain, that was what broke me. The lack of courtesy to even hear me out broke me. Certainly there were a million other cracks that made me eventually snap, but on October 25, 2013, I knew there was no going back. I dropped everything at that moment, went to my son's school, and enjoyed his program with full attention. As soon as the program ended, I called my direct boss, explained what had happened, and told him how furious I was. While he understood my frustration, I sensed he did not have much control over the situation (too many complaints back to the boss about this type of behavior and how it must change), and I realized that, if I wanted change, I had to be the one to seek it. I had to evaluate my worth and potential, and de-termine whether I was deserving of this silly and bewildering treatment. I had to determine whether the impact I so wanted, that I promised myself after 9/11 and as a young idealistic woman, was something I could achieve or not. The only way I would ever know is if I found it myself.

Clearly the years of seeking that "to be determined" impact through other means, working with decision makers whose opinions I either did not always agree with or, in some cases, disrespected, had not cut it for me. I could either continue talking about making a difference, or I could go out and actually make the difference by my actions.

—

The next day was a Friday. As soon as I got to the office, I went to speak to my boss. While it may not have been the best decision for my family (um, no more paychecks? What about insurance?), I quit. I gave the NGO 60 days to work with me and wrap up anything left hanging, but I told my boss I was done trying to make this situation work for me any longer. My boss laughed. I was not laughing. He thought I was just acting emotionally. I told him I was serious. And, in that moment, I decided how I would spend the rest of my adult life—working for no one except the people who need my help the most—the people in struggling communities who desperately need an interjection of help, hope, and love.

—

After a bit more discussion, my boss realized that I was indeed serious about this. He could tell that the months of anger, dissatisfaction, and frustration were culminating in this moment. We agreed to the terms of my 60-day resignation and I left.

As soon as I walked out of my boss' office, I felt freedom. I was awash in gratitude that the time had come. I had no idea what I was going to do, or how I would help support my family, but I still felt an inexplicable peace. I had this innate sense that I was heading in the right direction, and toward my end goal of impact and fulfillment. I was untethered from the anger and frustration immediately and reveled in the positive aura almost instantaneously. I knew we would be okay as a family, despite financial challenges or moments of uncertainty; I was giddy with excitement and joy.

That night I came home to my husband so that we could discuss what my resigning would do for our finances, insurance, the children's school fees, etc. I suggested the idea of starting my own company. We agreed that I should explore this over the next 60 days, which I committed to doing. Over the next few days, I dusted off the notes I had taken while in New England, started examining the analysis I had done on consulting companies working in sustainability, impact partnerships, and collaboration, and started writing my business plan. The content flowed easily and I could barely sleep with such determination racing through my blood. This was going to be my future, it was going to be successful, and it was going to deliver impact.

That much I knew.

BOTTOM LINE:

When change seems inevitable, and you suspect that something must give, trust your intuition and value your worth higher than the alternative of the status quo. Everything does happen for a reason, and despite challenges that may arise, hard work and contributing to a greater good will bring about peace and satisfaction. It will be okay because you are in charge of your path, your impact, and your decision-making.

10

Making Connective Impact

As I child, I loved visiting my father's office. He allowed me to stuff envelopes, remove staples, or, if I was lucky, type letters. Being at Dad's office felt like the best kind of adventure. I felt a sense of energy and excitement just as I did when I would play office with my neighbors growing up.

My father spent 30 years working as a businessman, despite starting his career as a lawyer. He had practiced law for five years and realized he wanted something different for his career and his personal life. He started working for his father and uncle at the family's plumbing tool manufacturing business—not sexy, but functional. Dad took over as President after my grandfather retired, and built the business into a very competitive and innovative supplier to some of the biggest retailers in the sector. While the plumbing industry did not interest him much, being a business owner did. Even after retiring, my father found a way to challenge himself, building a lucrative Russian Avant Garde art business, fulfilling a passion he developed during his travels in college. At the age of 67, he is still flourishing as an art dealer, perhaps even more successfully than as a businessman. His passion and drive are inspiring. My father would often say that, like him, I would own a business someday, and I would find a way to support myself drawing from what excites or drives me. When he said that, I wondered what that would look like or if that could ever happen. It sounded wonderful though, and based on how successful my dad was (and still is), I thought that should be a goal of mine, too.

As a child, I also spent many a school break helping my mother in her classroom. For more than 30 years, my mom taught at a private elementary school down the street from my own. Our schools were technically "rivals," but I was so proud of the children my mom taught and the futures she shaped. Her passion for helping others resonated with me at a very early age, and I still remember overhearing my mom tell stories about families who were struggling to keep their children in private school because of the high cost, or had challenges with their marriages, disabilities, emotional instability, or illness. My mother handled these issues with grace. Like my father, I assumed I would own my own business someday. It was inevitable that my career would imbed caring for others as a priority, too, like it was (and still very much is) for my mother.

When the time came to consider what was next after my resignation, though, I still thought starting my own company was crazy. A desire to effect change and be fulfilled was a priority, but the thought of building my own path, instead of following others on theirs, was overwhelming and scary. As I began to revisit the business plan I had roughly begun while in New England, I started to see more clearly what was needed to make social, environmental, and economic impact more definitive. I could barely sleep some nights as thoughts and inspired ideas raced through my mind. I reached out to many of my contacts, asking them their thoughts about some of my initial ideas, and also spent time learning from other consultants about how they started their own businesses.

My fear and vulnerability quickly morphed into pure excitement. Maybe I really did have something to offer! I knew there was something missing in the space of sustainability, and I could work to fill that gap! It took putting myself out there in ways I was not completely comfortable with to find what niche I could fill, and how someone with my skillset could not only be helpful, but could also bring in an income. It's one thing to be offering a service; it's a completely other thing to charge for it!

—

I spent the 60 days between my resignation and my last day at the NGO fleshing out my business plan, researching different consulting models, talking to attorneys and accountants, and learning as much as I could about being an entrepreneur. Luckily, there is so much insight and knowledge to be shared that it was easy for me to find resources. The challenge became shifting through everything and narrowing my focus onto what I was truly capable to do.

Along with this period, though, came a very harsh reality about finances. I was lucky to have a bit of savings and a small injection from my parents to get me started, which many entrepreneurs do not have. I figured I had enough to get me started and perhaps into about two to three months of working without adding income to our household. That would not be a very long period to go without work, but I had faith that, with the right balance of networking and hard-to-the-bone work, I would find some way of bringing in some money.

—

In addition to doing the usual business-launching prep work, including building a website, incorporating as an LLC, and creating financial forecasts, I also had to establish a name that would set me apart. I was not into the idea of Joanne Sonenshine Consulting. I wanted to evoke the reality that this business was more than just me. I wanted a business that had relevance without my name attached to it, so others could take any lessons I learned, or work I produced, and make it their own. I wanted my practice to be open source so my process of connecting partners and establishing effective collaborations would be replicable, scalable, and useful to anyone who needed it. The business, at its core, would be about making change lasting, and I wanted to be clear from the outset that nothing would get in the way of that—certainly not me. I had spent too many years trying to build a sustainable future for communities of need by attaching a complicated organizational mission to it.

I created a mission that was pure and simple: *To aid organizations in collaborative goal development, partnership strategy, coalition building and fundraising in order to solve some of the most complex problems of our time.* I planned to work with organizations—public, private, government, whatever—that were committed to making the world a better place. I wanted the luxury of picking and choosing which organizations I would work with, because I wanted to be sure I was prioritizing the work, not the brand, not the money, nor the perception. I was going to be selective and work with organizations committed to solving a problem plaguing our planet. I also set out to prioritize risk-taking, honesty, and transparency in my engagements with each client. My approach would be to connect organizations with each other in order to make solving these problems more streamlined, efficient, and effective.

—

Partnership and collaboration had been hot-button trends for a while, and I saw no letting up. In my experiences through government, the private sector, and at the NGO, though, I often saw partnership development handled wrong, the proper pre-work incomplete. I considered partnership as one would consider dating. There needs to be vetting, a few first dates, and perhaps a matchmaker, someone like me, who could help navigate the pluses and minuses of each potential partner. I wanted to be the center point that helped organizations pick the most effective partners for their goals, and then align those goals so the solutions were mutually beneficial, not just one-sided. In essence, I wanted to fix many of the problems I had uncovered over my years of working in sustainability: wasted money, too much time taken to get work underway, overlapping priorities that lack comparative advantage, inefficiency, and, in many cases, too little impact. I wanted to find the right connections for impact and just do good work!

One night, as I was tossing and turning over potential company names, I started jotting down what approaches to collaboration best suited this frame of reference I was building. The method that had resonated with me most was developed by the consulting company, FSG, founded by famed Harvard economist Michael Porter and philanthropist Mark Kramer. It is called Collective Impact, and it "occurs when organizations from different sectors agree to solve a specific social problem using a common agenda, aligning their efforts, and using common measures of success."[9]

I appreciated that utilizing Collective Impact methods for collaboration allowed each participant to take on an individualized role contributing to a greater goal, yet still be guided by clear direction and responsibilities. What was often missing in development was clarity around who was responsible for what delivery, what measurement, what funding, and what partnerships. After learning about Collective Impact over the years, it made sense to me as a solution to some of development's largest problems. That said, I often wondered if Collective Impact was missing a critical first step: It would not be successful if the members of the collaboration were not the best chosen for the particular goal. Finding the right balance between qualities and characteristics of each organization was just as critical to a collaboration as the end result itself.

Thus, while I knew I wanted to utilize a method of collective impact in my collaboration work to improve development, I also knew that finding the right connections, and establishing real relationships between each party or partner would be even more important and critical for successful outcomes. Collective Impact, just built with the proper connections. Connective Impact! It came to me in the middle of the night as I was running all of these scenarios through my head. My company was born.

—

I launched Connective Impact on January 15, 2014. It was a proud moment, representing years of struggle to find a career identity that brought fulfillment, but also allowed me to stay true to my word that lasting change was my primary mover. In operating independently, and seeking work with substantive impact, I have found a joy that is unlike any professional experience yet. I can take risks, be honest to company leaders about what they must do to be true corporate citizens, put aside titles, and focus on what makes each person tick, find their inner steward, and drill down the mechanics of not just the organizations that want to effect change, but the people within them who want to deliver impact for personal fulfillment as well.

In essence, I am able to recognize the challenges within each of my clients that I faced when I was in their shoes, and hopefully make it easier for each of the individuals that I work with, and have come to know and respect, to make decisions that have positive consequences for the people of our planet, and the environment around us.

In the same way, I hope to draw out what fulfills each of my clients (as it relates to their organizational social, environmental, and economic impact goals), I am able to find legitimate partnerships and build collaborations that are born of transparency, commitment, and delivery of impact based on mutual aims of effecting change. By prioritizing effective matchmaking, I am helping my clients leap over the hurdles that I struggled with year after year. It is not by accident that I went through all of the challenges I did. Each struggle helped me think about what makes partnership for impact successful or not. In the end, I realized it takes just six steps to find a scenario for collaboration that can be successful.

—

So how does an organization go through a process of "connective" impact?

- First, the organization must prioritize its own goals and understand the space in which its goals are achievable. This is important for getting a broad view of longer-term thinking, where current challenges are, where opportunities are, and where organizations see partnering as helping or adding value. In some cases, it is important to consider the extent to which existing partnerships or engagements are working, to determine where change is needed.

  For companies, there is a reality that cannot be ignored here: Making impact at the bottom line is also a priority. As a champion for business as a force for good, I never ignore that important point. Part of my engagement with NGOs is making sure they understand this before working with companies. Linking the work to the business outcomes ensures the development result is longer-lasting and more impactful. It is also a way to build the infrastructure across communities and prepare them for future development.

- Next, it is critical to determine whether the goal(s) can be achieved alone or is dependent on others. I would argue that, almost always, true aspirational social impact goals MUST involve others. Sometimes, though, organizations or individuals need more time to work through their own goal development before considering partnering or collaboration.

- Then comes one of the more difficult steps. Organizations need to understand the other players and their roles. Who are potential collaborators? What groups are already out there? Where is the best place to start any effort? At this stage, finding an appropriate connector to coordinate teams, develop strategies around collective impact, and measure results is critical (this is where Connective Impact's largest role is played).

In my more than 15 years working with companies and other organizations around corporate social responsibility, environmental impact, and sustainability, what I notice time and again is the fortitude born by group action. We need to know who is out there, what they are doing, and how we can contribute to each other's missions. We need to make strong linkages, and find the right chains to attach ourselves. Ensuring no duplication and making investments efficient is dependent on proper coordination here.

- Once collaborations are established, and partnerships defined, there are two key next steps that are often ignored in the space of finding impact:

  o First, organizations must monitor their progress across partnerships and collaborations to be sure they are paying their dues and providing a return on the investment.

  o Second, organizations must go into a redefine stage where they ensure partnerships are moving in the right direction or correcting any scenarios where they aren't.

This process can be adjusted for nearly any situation where mutual goal development is needed (including in determining whether a job is suitable, a location move makes sense, or even whether to see your first date again)! In many ways, these six steps mirror the processes I had to go through to determine where I would find fulfillment in my career and personal future. I had to take stock of my own needs first, consider what was out there, what had not worked, and what was the opportunity for me. From there I had to consider what professional space was open for me and where I could add value. I will always be in the tweaking phase, continually addressing changes as they arise to make my company most valuable to my clients and the work most impactful.

—

About a month after launching Connective Impact, I flew back to the Northeastern city by the lake to present my business concept to my friends at the company whose sustainability advisory I had been on before I left the NGO. This time, while I took my walk around the crystal clear lake, conceptualizing the future for Connective Impact, not only did I make a tour around the company offices on that lake, but I held meetings with executives at each one, sharing my new concept around Connective Impact, providing input and advising on how their companies could add value to existing partnerships, and bring greater impact to their work by establishing new partnerships. I did this without holding back, by taking some risks, and sharing my opinions outright. It was liberating, it was meaningful, and man, was it fulfilling.

—

It took me about six weeks to find my first paying client. While it was scary to be financially strapped for a couple of months, the response to my concept was positive from day one. I have not encountered one person who, in hearing about my approach, has discounted it or said it was not valuable. In contrast, I have received a lot of positive feedback on what Connective Impact aims to achieve, and have full confidence that the work we are doing now will continue to be relevant and necessary into the future.

—

One of the most critical elements supporting my work now is managing my network and relationships. I often tell anyone who will listen that it pays to keep in contact with anyone who has been part of a professional or personal past. It always amazes me how often paths crisscross and reattach in different ways. I have been able to reconnect with so many past colleagues over the last few years, and it helps keep me learning, inspired, and curious. You never know when someone in your network can be of help, and everyone really does like to help each other!

One of the biggest pieces of advice I give young professionals is to network the hell out of their time. You can never have too many entry points into organizations you want to learn more about, work with, or be employed by. Utilizing contacts makes those processes much easier, and it saves time for everyone involved. Building on my network from the last 15 years, I have been incredibly grateful to work with some of the most innovative, proactive, and impactful companies, NGOs, and organizations in the space of social, environmental, and economic impact since launching. I have been able to say "no" to organizations whose missions I did not agree with or respect. And I have been able to find true impact by being honest, transparent, real, and focused. My path to impact was not straight, or too fast or too slow. It was a circuitous journey unlike anyone else's and each step along the way, while challenging at times, and rewarding at others, brought me to the place of content and fulfillment of today.

BOTTOM LINE:

When seeking a path to impact, one almost always questions if the direction is correct, or if decisions are the right ones. Building relationships, testing the waters, asking questions, and being curious will help you find your impact and correct path. There is not only one way of doing things, and your trajectory will be what it will be as long as you trust in yourself that you are taking risks and listening to your instinct. Focusing on what makes you feel joy and passion, and what brings you fulfillment, even if in pieces bit by bit, will take you far, and finding the right partners, colleagues, guides, and listening to your inner voice will get you where you need to be.

Epilogue

When sharing both my impetus and rationale for writing this book, I heard countless stories of those who faced similar existential questions about how to find fulfillment and meaning in a career path that seems, in many ways, either preordained or dictated by variables that were out of their control.

During one conversation with my friend, Ann, she shared with me a commencement speech she gave at her alma mater, the Jackson School of International Studies at the University of Washington. Interestingly, the speech was given at the Center for Spiritual Living, which is notable in that, for many, certainly for me, the path to finding fulfillment is very much akin to one people may take to find spirituality or religion.

In her speech, Ann insinuated that paths are often meandering because most people do not start out their careers knowing exactly what they want to do with their lives, nor the steps they need to take to get there. She continues by sharing the honesty and raw reality that "clarity of vision and purpose...is rare." By telling the students in the audience that taking a meandering path is not only okay, but recommended, she allows them the space to realize that it is okay to not have everything figured out. That being comfortable with the discomfort of not knowing what the future holds is actually a good thing. It allows room for exploration and creativity in decision-making so each step along the path can take you either left, right, or center toward true fulfillment.

—

By writing this book, I share my journey in the hopes of inspiring my readers to seek greater impact in the work they do, the life they lead, and decisions they make. Perhaps by reading about my experiences, and those of others whose passions and inner guides have taken them on differing paths to finding fulfillment and impact, those who are in a similar life-shifting scenario can gain solace that they are not alone in the feelings of fear, trepidation, and weariness. There are options to find what fits for your life, by trusting instincts, taking risks, being comfortable with saying "no" when appropriate, and being true about who you are and what you want out of life.

In no way do I claim to have all the answers. If I did, that would mean my journey was complete, and I certainly hope it has only just begun for me. Although the process to get to where I am now, to find fulfillment in my career, and satisfaction in my commitments, was neither quick nor easy, I imagine that there is way more in store for me as I continue down the path with Connective Impact. We all have different paths we can take, and decisions are part of the approach that guide us. Ignore those who doubt you, test new ways of doing what you've always done, and look for the best in what relationships can provide. Make the most of every situation you are in, learn deeply, and take steps forward, even if they seem minor. Always be curious and ask questions. Manage your network and keep tabs on everyone who can be of help as you figure out what comes next for you. Don't get discouraged if you think you have veered in a different direction. Remember that there is a reason you think the way you do and make decisions the way you do. While you may feel you are losing your way, don't stop moving forward. Go forth with what feels right, be real, and be you.

Bottom Lines

BOTTOM LINE #1:

There is no one path to fulfillment. Your individual journey could be a marathon, a series of short sprints, or even several loops around the same track. There is no one way forward. What matters is that you always question where you are headed and why. Don't be afraid to challenge those in "authority" positions, and question everything. Be curious, be brave, and find your passion.

BOTTOM LINE #2:

Making a difference means different things to different people. Everyone finds their fulfillment in different ways, at different speeds, and through various journeys. You may find that what you were looking for all along was the purpose of the journey in the first place. Follow your instincts, trust yourself, and find the confidence to test assumptions.

BOTTOM LINE #3:

Expectations can lead to feelings of frustration, dissatisfaction, and regret. You design your path based on the expectations of those around you, but it should be based equally (and maybe even more so) on what you feel, where you see need, where you provide value, and where you can have the most impact.

BOTTOM LINE #4:

Unexpected turns can shift your goals, aspirations, and actions. Circumstances have meaning and can be your best ally as you seek personal fulfillment. Making the most out of tragedies, challenges, existential questions, or personal difficulty forces us to stay human, but can also shape a more meaningful and measurable outcome.

BOTTOM LINE #5:

The experience of changing direction and finding alternative routes to fulfillment can be rife with challenges and setbacks, difficulties, self-doubt, frustration, and a wish that time would move faster. During this time you must keep going, try different things, learn from those around you, build your network, build relationships, determine where you feel success, what makes you tick, and eliminate what brings you down.

BOTTOM LINE #6:

While seeking fulfillment, it is critical to be persistent and focused on building relationships with those who have mutual interests. Focus on what value you can bring to those doing the work that inspires you. We are all just looking for a way to make our path have meaning.

BOTTOM LINE #7:

It may be unrealistic to assume that balancing personal demands, obligations, interests, and the needs of your family will be unrelated to how you seek fulfillment and deliver impact. Stay true to your mission, and hold onto the hope that you will find the way through. You may have to make tough choices, but keep focusing on what drives you, ignoring the naysayers and continually moving forward.

BOTTOM LINE #8:

Risk taking is different for everyone. Yet, by taking risks and stepping outside of your comfort zone, you can effect change and make significant impact. Without taking risks or confronting fears of failure, vulnerability, or seeing your true self, your potential impact is thwarted and fulfillment is squandered. Expect for yourself only the best, and that is what you will get. Your own expectations will help you set your path and determine the way forward.

BOTTOM LINE #9:

When change seems inevitable, and you suspect that something must give, trust your intuition and value your worth higher than the alternative of the status quo. Everything does happen for a reason, and despite challenges that may arise, hard work and contributing to a greater good will bring about peace and satisfaction. It will be okay because you are in charge of your path, your impact, and your decision-making.

BOTTOM LINE #10:

When seeking a path to impact, one almost always questions if the direction is correct, or if decisions are the right ones. Building relationships, testing the waters, asking questions, and being curious will help you find your impact and correct path. There is not only one way of doing things, and your trajectory will be what it will be as long as you trust in yourself that you are taking risks and listening to your instinct. Focusing on what makes you feel joy and passion, and what brings you fulfillment, even if in pieces bit by bit, will take you far, and finding the right partners, colleagues, guides, and listening to your inner voice will get you where you need to be.

Acknowledgments

In writing this book, I hope to acknowledge the millions of people living in dire circumstances, and whose lives can and will be made better by the change seekers among us.

A special thank you to Senthil Nathan, Pierre Ferrari, Michael Jones, Ken Lander, Lorna Davis, Lucy Helm, and Trevor Waldock, for sharing your heroic adventures and inspiring stories with me and the masses as a way to encourage change-seeking and impact-making. I am grateful for your time and commitment to this book and the amazing work each of you does to make the world a more productive, peaceful, and content place to live.

I could not have started down this path of storytelling if it weren't for the encouragement of my friend, Adam Gropper, author of *Making Partner: The Essential Guide to Negotiating the Law School Path and Beyond*. Adam was the first to convince me that I had the potential to be an author just like him, and that it was all there inside, waiting to bubble up. Thanks to Adam, his wife and my friend, Amy, and a few glasses of wine, this book is here today.

As a first-time author, I had no preconceived notions about writing a book, and felt quite apprehensive at the onset. The team at Elevate Publishing could not have been more patient with me, and provided me a sense of comfort at each step along the way. I cannot thank you enough for sticking with me and keeping me focused, on task and making me feel like I mattered.

I want to thank Anna McHargue, especially. As my editor she received the brunt of my silly questions, and yet she never once made me question my rationale for writing this book. On the contrary Anna kept me inspired, writing feverishly to address her questions, and sent virtual pats on the back just when I needed them. A kindred spirit, no question, and I am so thankful to have met her through this process.

To my family: Mom and Dad—your unwavering support and constant guidance have fueled me for four decades now, and I cannot thank you enough for every ounce of your love. I am who I am because of you, and I can't think of two better people to teach me everything I know. Nancy, Gerald, and Emily—you have been true cheerleaders of this project. Thank you for all of the positive encouragement along the way.

To the best friends and lifelines a girl could ask for (Carin P., Carin J., Jessica, Rachel, Alison, Sarah L., Karen, Joy, Sarah A., Erin, Hallee, Kim, and Sarah K.), your friendships keep me going despite every crazy moment of my life, and I am so grateful to each of you.

As someone who moves fast and furiously, I am lucky to have a steadfast and committed partner in my husband, David Sonenshine. Thank you for laughing with me just when

I need it most, learning with me as we struggle to be good, kind, and responsible adults, and taking this crazy journey of life with me especially when I tend to add a lot of the craziness to the journey. Although Oprah never shared the story of how we met on her show as I hoped she would, it is still one of the greatest miracles in my life.

Last, but never least, I want to thank the two people who challenge me to be better every day of my life: Jacob and Daniel. By seeing the world through your eyes, you help me seek out ways to change the world for the better, so you and your futures are filled with only happiness and beauty. You may be too young to read this book now, but I hope that one day you do, and you see me and my hope for your lives in a different way than before. I love you both with every bone in my body. And then some.

Thank you to everyone who contributed to this book, near and far. Thank you to those reading it. May we find the strength and resolute action to effect change together.

Endnotes

[1] Novogratz, Jaqueline, *The Blue Sweater*. (New York, Rodale Books, 2009), pp. 196.

[2] Novogratz, Jaqueline, *The Blue Sweater*. (New York, Rodale Books, 2009), pp. 4.

[3] Slade, Holie. (2014, March). Why This Man Gave Up His $40M Company To 'Fix' Coffee. *Forbes*.

[4] Rubin, Robert. *In an Uncertain World: Tough Choices from Wall Street to Washington*. (New York, Random House, 2003) pp. 64.

[5] Bronson, Po. What Should I Do With My Life (New York, Random House, 2002), pp xv.

[6] Bronson, Po. What Should I Do With My Life (New York, Random House, 2002), pp 3.

[7] https://www.edf.org/partnerships/mcdonalds

[8] http://www.theatlantic.com/magazine/archive/2012/07/why-women-still-cant-have-it-all/309020/

[9] http://www.fsg.org/ideas-in-action/collective-impact

JOANNE SONENSHINE is Founder + CEO of
Connective Impact, an advisory firm aiding
organizations in strategic goal development,
partnership strategy, fundraising diversifi-
cation, and collective thinking in order to
solve some of the most complex problems of
our time. Originally from Cleveland, Ohio,
Joanne is a trained development economist
and has been living and working in the
Washington, D.C. area since 2004. Her professional experiences have included working
at the U.S. Department of Commerce International Trade Association, as a registered
lobbyist advocating for more comprehensive
environmental sustainability regulations, and
as a program director for a large international
NGO working on climate change, land use,
and agriculture investments. Joanne lives in
Arlington, Virginia, with her husband and
two boys.

elevate
publishing

**DELIVERING TRANSFORMATIVE MESSAGES
TO THE WORLD**

Visit www.elevatepub.com for our latest offerings.

NO TREES WERE HARMED IN THE MAKING OF THIS BOOK.

Okay, so a few did make the ultimate sacrifice.

In order to steward our environment, we are partnered with *Plant With Purpose*, to plant a tree for every tree that paid the price for the printing of this book.

To learn more, visit www.elevatepub.com/about

PLANT WITH PURPOSE | WWW.PLANTWITHPURPOSE.ORG